Jacqueline Holzman
Mayor - Ottawa 1991 - 1997
Chair Ottawa Congress Centre 1998 - 2003

OTTAWA
THEN & NOW

FOR THE PEOPLE WHO HAVE MADE THIS CITY GREAT, AND THOSE WHO CONTINUE TO DO SO.

FOR GEORGE AND ELSIE, WHO ALSO MADE OTTAWA HOME.

FOR WINONA, WHO LIVED HER BEAUTIFUL LIFE ALONG THE OTTAWA.

AND FOR CHANTAL.

No other nation's state edifices can boast a more spectacular site than these high bluffs occupied by Canada's neo-gothic Parliament Buildings. Only three decades ago, this scene was also one of vibrant industry – complete with log booms, tugs and the ever present sounds and smells of a thriving lumber town. Now the sunny shores of Entrance Bay are accessed by cyclists and tourists, who find their way down to the water's edge via the Rideau Canal locks or the pathways that follow the river.

Known as the second coldest national capital in the world, Ottawa can be a harsh and forbidding place when the fierce winds of winter come. Now the waters of Entrance Bay are frozen two feet thick and both the Rideau Canal locks and Chateau Laurier Hotel are lost from sight in the driving snow. The freshly fallen snow obscures the embankment where the river ends and the grounds of the Canadian Museum of Civilization begin.

Ottawa, Then and Now

By: Jacquelin Holzman and Rosalind Tosh
Photography: John McQuarrie

Published by: Magic Light Publishing
                    John McQuarrie Photography
                    192 Bruyere Street
                    Ottawa, Ontario
                    K1N 5E1

                    (613) 241-1833
                    FAX: 241-2085
                    e-mail: mcq@magma.ca

For reproductions of John's photographs call Love Visuals at:
                    (613) 824-8608
                    e-mail: love@magma.ca

Design: Dave O'Malley and John McQuarrie
Captions: Dave O'Malley
Production   James Jones, Aerographics
Printing: Digital Prepress & Printing Professional Ltd.
                Hong Kong

Canadian Cataloguing in Publication Data

Holzman, Jacquelin
  Ottawa, then & now

ISBN 0-9699761-5-1

1. National Capital Region (Canada)--History--Pictorial
works, I. McQuarrie, John, 1946- II. Tosh, Rosalind
III. Title. IV. Title: Ottawa, then and now.

FC2787.H64 1999   971.3'83'00222   C99-900468-9
F1059.5.09H65 1999

Printed and bound in China

Contents

Parliament Hill, Major's Hill Park (lower right) and the barricaded streets of downtown Ottawa teem with boisterous and sun-burnt Canadians eager for the coming Canada Day extravaganza and fireworks display. A hot air balloon in the shape of a giant Mountie and his charger drifts silently above the spot where, 125 years before, the North West Mounted Police was created.

AUTHORS' INTRODUCTION

JACQUELIN HOLZMAN Serendipity is not always arbitrary. When fortune selected Ottawa – an unlikely frontier town in the middle of nowhere and with a somewhat checkered history – to be the capital city of Canada in 1859, she knew very well what she was doing. The passage of time since then has proven her choice to have been a most happy one.

Random luck, however, made it my own good fortune to be able to claim Ottawa as my home town. A young graduate from the University of Manitoba, my father was invited by Metropolitan Life to come to Ottawa to establish their actuarial department in the early '30s. He and his bride accepted that offer and I am thankful for it every day. The nature and amenities of this international city with the heart of a small town have ensured a life that is enriching, fulfilling and most agreeable – and to be able to share these same assets with my own children, and now their children, has been nothing short of phenomenal.

It seems that I have been allotted a very large share of good fortune because, from 1991 to 1997, I was granted the incredible privilege of serving this wonderful city as Mayor. I couldn't have imagined a more welcome turn of events. The opportunity to return to my community even a fraction of the gifts it has given me filled me with gratitude and immense satisfaction. What a bonus!

You will discover as you read this book just how powerful chance, luck, fate and fortune are, not only in our individual lives but also in shaping the destiny – and destining the shape – of the little community that grew into the capital city of the largest democracy in the modern world.

ROSALIND TOSH Sight unseen and from an ocean away, I chose beautiful Ottawa as my home a full ten years before I arrived here. I believed in trusting my instinct.

Born in a capital city – Belfast – and energized by the intellectual perks that come with a town of capital status, I knew Ottawa would be the place for me when the time came to leave my native land. My first companion-in-adventure, however, chose Paris, France instead and I had to wait. A year later, I introduced a second friend to the Canadian Consul (who then asked if I was recruiting immigrants!) and this time my dream came one step closer to fruition: I got as far as Toronto. One husband, two children and eight years later, Ottawa finally became my home.

Ask me where my roots are and I'll say, without hesitation, Ottawa. It is in this city of great natural beauty, enriching lifestyle, and water – glorious water – that I have been most meaningfully challenged and stimulated for two-and-a-half decades. And the act of researching this book, of coming to know Ottawa's fascinating history, has been the icing on the cake. Now, when I pass landmarks, I celebrate their local, national and international significance and, equally as compelling, I marvel at what they might have become had the quirks of history played out another way.

This wonderful sense of familiarity deepens my sense of belonging, of being truly home. For this, I thank John McQuarrie (a gifted and perceptive artist, whose idea this book was), Jacquelin Holzman (the consummate champion and lover of everything to do with this city), Dave O'Malley (who knows instinctively how to set a jewel to best advantage) and Louise Roy-Brochu (City of Ottawa Archivist Extraordinaire).

I still believe in trusting my instinct. I have not been disappointed.

The Alexandra Bridge, also known as the Interprovincial Bridge, was the second to join Ottawa and Hull, Québec. Built originally as a combination carriage and railway bridge, the Interprovincial had a single track down the centre and vehicle lanes on each side. Trains left Union Station via a short tunnel under Wellington Street's Plaza Bridge and emerged below the Chateau Laurier following the curve of the cliffs overlooking the locks. The west lane of the bridge, which once rumbled to the sounds of Ottawa-bound traffic, now carries pedestrians in both directions between downtown Ottawa and the Canadian Museum of Civilization (centre). There is no better vantagepoint from which to view the entire panorama of locks, Parliament Hill, Ottawa River and the skylines of both cities. To the west (left), we can still see the remnants of the huge pulp and paper mills of E.B. Eddy, which dominated the Hull skyline for over a century.

INTRODUCTION

In the Spring of 1800, the world's attention was focused on Napoleon, as he consolidated his conquest of Italy. That same spring, far from the eye of the world, a visionary American from Boston had begun clearing land to build a settlement he would call Wrightstown, beside the Chaudière Falls, where the city of Hull, Quebec now stands. Philemon Wright's original group would, 200 years later, have grown to a National Capital with a population of some 500,000 people.

Now imagine you could time-travel back to a cold winter night in 1826, walking into Wright's Tavern at Chaudière Falls. There you spot Colonel By himself, the English soldier charged with building a canal to Kingston, in conversation with Wright. And further imagine joining these men with your copy of this book in hand. By candlelight, you give them a tantalizing glimpse of what is to come. Or perhaps the year of your journey is 1868 and you run into Sir John A. Macdonald, Canada's first Prime Minister, along with Lord Monck, the first Governor General, at a reception celebrating the opening of Rideau Hall. Picture their reaction as you show them the Capital they were helping to shape.

While time travel is an adventure that belongs to the future, we hope you will find our 200-year retrospective within these pages the next best thing. For here is Ottawa like you have never seen her before. You will be present at her birth in a virgin wilderness and, from the comfort of your favourite chair, watch her growth through two centuries to the point where she is poised to begin a third century in a world entering its third millennium. An intimate portrait of many of the places that define the capital, her businesses, culture, recreation, architecture, parks, homes, schools, transportation systems and people emerging from virgin forest to thriving city.

For this photographer, it was love at first sight. The year was 1956 and the train delivering our family from Kentville, Nova Scotia to an exciting new home in Ottawa had just embarked on her crossing of the Alexandra Bridge from Hull. That first sight of Parliament Hill gliding past the bridge girders is still etched in my mind. Here was the capital of my country and nine year-old eyes were popping. This was the first time I had actually looked upon a sight that I had seen in a book. And today, over forty years later, the view from the walkway of that same bridge still gives me goosebumps and continues to fuel my ardour for my favourite place on Earth.

John McQuarrie
Photographer and Publisher

The Royal initials of E II R – Elizabeth II, Queen of the British Commonwealth gleam on the polished mace of the Drum Major of the Governor General's Foot Guards. In the dome under the miniature St. Edward's Crown (worn by reigning British Monarchs at their coronations), we see the reflection of the Parliament Buildings where, each day throughout the summer, this busby-wearing drum major and his impeccably turned out Guardsmen keep alive a tradition that has belonged to this city since the beginning of Confederation.

One had to be of adventurous spirit to take on the mighty Ottawa in the 17th and 18th centuries. The voyageurs, who opened up the vast lands to the north and west, brought their furs down the Ottawa to Montreal, to be shipped to fashionable Europeans. While they prided themselves with their excellent handling of their massive "canôts du nord", they didn't think twice about putting ashore to portage around the Chaudière.

THE FALLS GIVE BIRTH TO THE BAY

A THREATENED AMBUSH AT OTTAWA'S CHAUDIÈRE FALLS DID NOT TAKE PLACE IN 1660, LEADING ULTIMATELY TO INTERNATIONAL TREACHERY AND THE CREATION OF CANADA'S OLDEST RETAIL TRADING COMPANY.

In the 17th century, the Algonquin Outaouais Indians and the French controlled the Ottawa River above the Chaudière Falls, while the lower reaches were subject to Iroquois and English forces. The lucrative fur trade was badly diminished as coureurs des bois working the pelt-rich lands of the upper river invariably ran afoul of the Iroquois blockade at the falls. In 1660, however, a couple of trappers managed to make it through without incident and paddled their precious cargo on to Quebec City. When Pierre Esprit Radisson and Médard Chouart des Groseilliers arrived there, they were not given the warm welcome they expected. Instead, their furs were confiscated, the two men were fined and des Groseilliers was jailed, all because they had made the expedition without the appropriate licence.

On returning to France, they were given no satisfaction for this harsh treatment and so, incensed, Radisson and des Groseilliers proceeded to England, France's long-time adversary, where they offered their services to King Charles II. Charles promptly consented to the formation of the Company of Adventurers Trading into Hudson's Bay, to be financed by British merchants and led by the two entrepreneurs.

And so it was that The Hudson's Bay Company – "The Bay" – was born on May 2nd, 1670 and still thrives today, almost three-and-a-half centuries later, thanks to one ambush that didn't take place at Ottawa's Chaudière Falls.

The Chaudière spawned the growth of more than just the Hudson's Bay Company. It provided the reason for entrepreneurs to put down roots along the banks of the Ottawa and to find ways in which to employ its power, bridge its chasm and serve its users. In 1867 (right), it was still a long way from being tamed.

THE SACRED

Sometime in the 17th or 18th century, intrepid "voyageurs" make camp along the banks of the Ottawa River. Sleeping under their large, birch bark canoes to protect themselves from the elements, these fur traders and their native counterparts traditionally made use of camp sites at the present day location of the Museum of Civilization and at Chaudière Falls.

Francis Anne Hopkins / NATIONAL ARCHIVES OF CANADA / C-002773

THE INTERIOR OF THE SLEEPING NORTH AMERICAN CONTINENT WAS MOST EASILY REACHED IN THE 17TH CENTURY BY AN ANCIENT ABORIGINAL "HIGHWAY" — THE OTTAWA RIVER, THE MIGHTY KITCHISIPPI, RIVER OF THE ALGONQUIN.

The river irresistibly beckoned European explorers, fur traders and missionaries along its 1280 kilometres (800 miles) from the St. Lawrence River, along the Ottawa and then via Lake Huron to the abundance of the Mississippi Valley, the vast plains of the north west and the rich potential of the Arctic and Pacific oceans. The "boiling cauldron" of Ottawa's thundering Chaudière Falls was an enforced rest stop along the way.

In the early part of the 17th century, Chaudière Falls (named after the French word for cauldron – a reference to the steamy mists that boiled off the raging water in winter) was still a wild and untamed torrent.

Samuel de Champlain, a French explorer, ventured far up what we now call the Ottawa River. He most certainly beached his expedition's canoes on the far side of the river, across from the bluffs of present-day Parliament Hill in order to scout the roaring tumult which lay to the west of him. His statue now stands atop Nepean Point, looking in that very direction.

The "chauldron" of the Chaudière Falls never failed to impress all who came upon it. The following is how Champlain first described it in 1613.

"A league thence we passed a rapid which is half a league wide and has a descent of six or seven fathoms. Here are many small islands which are nothing more than rough, steep rocks, covered with poor, scrubby wood. At one place the water falls with such force upon a rock that with the lapse of time it has hollowed out a wide, deep basin. Herein the water whirls around to such an extent, and in the middle sends up such big swirls, that the Indians call it Asticou, which means 'boiler'. This waterfall makes such a noise in this basin that it can be heard for more than two leagues away."

* A league is about 5 kilometers (3 miles) while a fathom is 6 feet.

Dams were built in the 19th century to control and employ the power of Chaudière Falls. From this spot grew the sprawling complex of saw, pulp and paper mills belonging to various lumber barons. Today, the last vestiges of these forest industries still operate around its fringes. The great expanse of open water upstream from the semicircular dam was once choked with logs waiting to be fed down the fast-moving log chutes. The hydroelectric potential of the falls still supplies electricity (bottom centre) for the E.B. Eddy facilities.

Looking northwest across the tamed Chaudière Falls to West Hull where, in 1800, Philemon Wright and his large entourage came to begin a new life. The building in the centre generates hydroelectric power for the last remaining E.B. Eddy mills (lower right) which still operate today.

Philemon Wright trudged 800 kilometres (500 miles) through snow and ice just to reach those falls on March 7th, 1800. He led his wife, their six children, five other families and 25 men from Massachusetts to homestead in the virgin forest on the north side of the cascading waters — waters so forceful that, in spring, they today generate electricity equal to one-tenth the power of an average nuclear reactor. Wright, lured by the political and social climate of Canada, had been smitten by the natural beauty of the area during earlier explorations. Indeed, "The imagination cannot picture anything so romantic," agreed Nicholas Garry, founder of the city of Winnipeg, when he visited Wright's settlement two decades later.

Buses and a streetcar of the Ottawa Transportation Commission await passengers at the foot of Eddy Street in Hull. Behind, stands the Ottawa House, an icon of Hull nightlife for generations, until it was levelled to make way for the federal office complex of Les Terrasses de la Chaudière. The 1950s saw an overlap of modern bus and antiquated streetcar service throughout the downtown core. By the 1960s, the trolleys and their tracks had all but disappeared, with only OTC buses servicing the watering holes across the river.

Looking straight down on the federal government complex known as Terrasse de la Chaudière, which houses the Department of Indian Affairs and Northern Development and Parks Canada, we are actually looking at the original site of Wrightstown close to where Philemon Wright's mill and tavern were located. Eddy Street (right) was still the heart of Hull's nightlife well into the 1970s with numerous and well-attended bars such as the Standish, the Rendezvous and the Ottawa House.

Philemon Wright knew a good location when he saw one. The American saw potential for a mill here at the edge of the tumbling water. The mill which was a going concern in this 1823 painting, would employ many of the men who came north with him. Hard work made for a thirsty man and Wright made back some of the wages he paid out at his tavern at the same location.

Wright's growing commerce brought him into partnerships with voyageurs and lumbermen. Here he is depicted completing an upstream portage in 1818 with a group of rugged voyageurs, as raftsmen take a faster but more dangerous route downstream through a stretch of white water. Wright wears a veil of mesh and long gloves to protect him from the scourge of black flies.

Wright's settlement spread to the riverbank on the Ontario side of the falls when construction of the Rideau Canal began in 1826. The city of Ottawa took root and flourished as the canal builders worked on this water highway, a long-planned route of safe passage for British troops after the St. Lawrence River became vulnerable in its role as the international boundary between British North America and its expansionist-minded neighbour to the south.

For many years, the locks at Entrance Bay were used only by commercial and military vessels. Nowadays they are employed only by pleasure craft making the climb or descent between the Ottawa River and the beautiful Rideau Waterway system, which ends 200 kilometers away at the Lake Ontario city of Kingston. These three views show a time lapse, as four pleasure boats are raised to the level of the last lock before entering the canal. The process of transiting the locks from the Ottawa River to the Rideau Canal eighty feet above, takes about two hours.

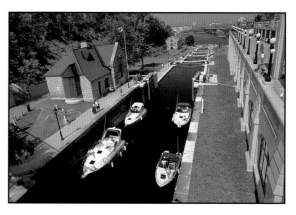

WHITE WATER RAFTING

The Ottawa River upstream from the Capital is now a water playground with several rafting tour operators offering the thrill of a lifetime. A professional rafter in the stern guides these adventurous tourists to the perfect spot over a ledge on the Ottawa River.

WHITE WATER RAFTING REAPS FORTUNES – BACK IN 1836

ROYALTY RISKED THE RAPIDS OF THE CHAUDIÈRE IN THE 19TH CENTURY, THRILLING TO THE EXHILARATION OF THE CITY'S FIRST TOURIST ATTRACTION.

Not for the faint of heart, the timber slide adventure began some 270 metres (900 feet) up-river from the falls and ran the rapids for more than a kilometre (three-quarters of a mile) between Victoria and Chaudière islands. The future King George V and Queen Mary of England and the Grand Duke Alexis of Russia were just some of the European royals who, like many common folk, came to "ride the slide" at Bytown.

Not all rafters make it downstream unscathed. Part of the fun is getting wet and for these folks it's an unscheduled dip in the cold Ottawa River.

The slide was built in 1836 to allow whole platforms of Ottawa Valley square timbers to negotiate the Chaudière Falls speedily and undamaged, trimming up-to-20 days off their journey down the Ottawa and St. Lawrence rivers to Quebec City. From there, as many as 1200 ships a season hurried the precious pine, oak and maple cargo to timber-hungry England and the fortunes of many an Ottawa entrepreneur were made. In fact, Ottawa quickly became known throughout the world by the peculiar – but fitting – title, Metropolis of Logs.

R. Pittaway / NATIONAL ARCHIVES OF CANADA / C-033339

The first eco-tourists? In 1901, citizens of Ottawa and Hull doff their hats as Their Royal Highnesses, the Duke and Duchess of Cornwall and York enjoy a raft ride of a different kind – a crib of specially prepared square timber. Lumbermen known as "raftsmen" routinely rode their timber rafts down the tumbling sluices of the Chaudière log slide on the south side of the Chaudière Falls.

It was Philemon Wright (who always seems to be avoiding the heavy work) who had the idea for the first square timber raft. Here, in 1809, he exhorts his starboard raftsmen to haul back on their oars to bring the ungainly craft (which Wright named Colombo*) under control.*

Charles William Jefferys / NATIONAL ARCHIVES OF CANADA / C073702

Napoleon Saves The Day

Napoleon Bonaparte was responsible for the success of the lumber trade which sustained the city of Ottawa through its infancy and childhood.

Philemon Wright spent every penny of his capital – a princely $20,000 – developing his community on the north side of the Ottawa River. His sawmill and grist mill were the first to harness the power of the Chaudière Falls and his hemp processing mill, tannery, blacksmith's shop, tailor's shop, shoe maker's shop and bakery ensured the comfort of the settlers. Now he needed a dependable source of export income to keep the community growing. The forests around him supplied the answer.

In 1805, ignoring the century-old wisdom that said it was impossible to navigate the Long Sault Rapids upstream from Montreal, Wright secured a contract to deliver 6000 oak staves to Quebec City by July 31st of the following year. He spent the fall and winter harvesting and preparing the shipment and, on June 11th, 1806, he and his men set out with a timber raft consisting of 700 logs, 9000 boards and the requisite oak staves. At the head of the Long Sault, they divided the raft into cribs of no more than 35 logs each and coaxed and bullied them through the raging waters. Many were smashed and lost and men risked their lives to pry open numerous quivering log jams. Finally, after 36 days, the Long Sault was conquered, the raft was re-assembled and the journey continued, though not without delays as the battered raft came apart several times en route.

Arriving in Quebec City on August 12 – 64 danger-filled days after leaving home – Wright was informed that his contract for the staves was null and void, due to late delivery. Furthermore, no one wanted his logs and boards. His brave gamble had blown up in his face and the future of his community was now in doubt. Thanks to Napoleon, however, he only had to wait three months for his luck to change. In November, in anticipation of Bonaparte's sealing off of the Baltic ports which were Britain's traditional source of timber, a fleet of British ships arrived in port, hungry for as much Canadian lumber as they could carry.

Though Philemon Wright was the man who opened the region for the logging industry, it was another American, by the name of Ezra Butler Eddy, who created an industrial legacy that lasts to this day at the Chaudière. In 1873, Eddy and his family, strike an aristocratic pose, befitting their baronial status. E.B., who would make such a physical impact on Canada's Capital, could trace his puritan lineage directly through his mother to Miles Standish of the 'Mayflower'.

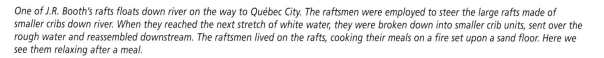

One of J.R. Booth's rafts floats down river on the way to Québec City. The raftsmen were employed to steer the large rafts made of smaller cribs down river. When they reached the next stretch of white water, they were broken down into smaller crib units, sent over the rough water and reassembled downstream. The raftsmen lived on the rafts, cooking their meals on a fire set upon a sand floor. Here we see them relaxing after a meal.

When word of the riches to be had in the wilds of the Ottawa Valley reached men with vision, they made haste to get in on the action. John Rudolphus Booth (right), from Waterloo, Québec, was a powerful man who made his enormous fortune on the backs of the lumbermen and raftsmen. Booth lost his own home in the Great Fire of 1900 as well as the entire contents of his lumberyard. It is a tribute to his tenacity and vigour at 72 when, upon hearing of the fire, he telegraphs his staff from Québec City, "Put out fire. Clear up debris. Prepare to rebuild. Will be home tomorrow." Now that's one tough man.

Boathouses and vegetation line the banks of the Rideau Canal just west of Bank Street in 1898. At right we can see a horse drawn buggy negotiating a dirt track that crosses the mouth of Brown's Inlet.

Today the same causeway has been expanded to accommodate the elegant roadway known as the Queen Elizabeth Driveway. The private boathouses have long since gone and the canal walls have been lined with concrete, but the large tree in the historic photograph still appears to be going strong in the modern photo. Stairs descend into the canal (which is in the process of being drained) in anticipation of winter, when thousands of skaters will make use of the world's longest ice skating rink.

Tour boats, like the Ottawa Queen, now ply the Rideau Canal from Union Station to Dow's Lake. The wide tour boats are specially designed to navigate the low clearance of the hydraulically lifted Pretoria Bridge.

At sunrise, a lone sculler from the Bytown Boat Club rows past the opening to Patterson Creek, one of two inlets which lead into the upscale community known as the Glebe.

For many, Bank Street is the most beautiful intersection of bridge and water along the entire Rideau system. In late August, hundreds of thousands of fairgoers, flocking to the Central Canada Exhibition at Lansdowne Park, enjoy the view in all directions.

24

Sister ship to the Ottawa Queen, Miss SBJ II comes to the end of her excursion as she prepares to pass beneath the MacKenzie King Bridge before docking at the old Union Station.

Three aerial views of the Rideau Canal today. At left, oarsmen in Royal Navy uniforms of the 1800s, re-enacting an historical scene for the annual Spring Flotilla, pass by the mouth of Patterson Creek. At centre, pedal boats, canoes and restaurant tables await the arrival of customers at the Dow's Lake Pavilion. In the 1980s the original wood frame pavilion still existed at this same location. At right, tourists taking a boat excursion on the canal enjoy the sunny stern deck as the boat begins its one hour tour.

Back in 1842, commercial river steamers made their landings at Fitzgibbon's Landing on the opposite side of the locks, where a road lead up the steep embankment to the heights known as Major's Hill. At right on the site of today's Parliament, we can see the military hospital that dominated the site at that time.

A sloop used for teaching youth about sailing tallships, steps her masts in readiness of an adventure on the spectacular Rideau Canal.

Down below on the Ottawa River, tour boats operate too. Popular for grad parties and tourists alike, the boats are considerably larger (two decks) than the canal boats. They take folks from the dock at the bottom of the locks around Entrance Bay, down river to Rideau Falls and then on to the mouth of the Gatineau River.

Water in the lowest lock overflows and spills into the Ottawa River. With Ottawa's modern skyline obscured by cliffs and trees, this scene would have looked much the same 150 years ago.

The building at the centre now houses the Bytown Museum, but once, as seen in the 1842 etching on the opposite page, it was the army commissariat.

Looking past the lockmasters house down the eight locks, the view has not changed much in the 150 years since Colonel By finished them.

Build it and they will come. Construction of the new Union Station is well under way by the summer of 1911. Forward thinking railroad people knew that when tourists, civil servants and businessmen alike alighted at the station, they would need a place to stay near the heart of downtown. What better place to construct their hotel than directly across Rideau Street. Behind the station's boxy form rises steel framework for the spires, turrets and mansards of the Chateau Laurier Hotel. The "Chateau"-style hotels were built by the Canadian Pacific and Canadian National Railways in every major city across the country from Québec City to Victoria. The "Chateau" is as much a part of the life and skyline of Ottawa as the Houses of Parliament. In this shot we can see the original tower, which burned to the ground with the Centre Block in 1916.

By the early 1920s, the station and hotel had been in operation for a decade. The long train sheds extend southward along the canal providing covered access to passenger cars in all types of weather. Much of the other side of the canal is given over to industry as well. The mounds along the edge are most likely gravel to be used for concrete in the construction of the Parliament Buildings, which now stand again in the distance. The unfinished Victory Memorial Tower, commemorating the end of the Great War, rises in the distance.

On a bright but frozen winter afternoon in 1927, a steam engine pulls a passenger train from its berth at Union Station. Through the great clouds of steam, we can now see that the Victory Memorial Tower is nearly complete. It was built in fits and starts over a number of years and by the time it was dedicated on Remembrance Day of the following year, it was renamed the Peace Tower.

All trains took on their passengers beneath the gloomy sheds, which were accessed through sliding grate doors inside the terminal. Some trains, bound for Québec and points east, entered the station on the two tracks on the left of the photo below. This enabled them to pull out of the station northward along the side of the locks, across the Interprovincial Bridge and on to their destinations. Prior to trains being brought into the sheds, mail cars were loaded on separate tracks to the right and were then shunted into the yard, where they were hooked to the appropriate outbound train. Postal Station "A" (behind smoke stack) was part of the downtown Ottawa skyline right up to the 1970s, when the central depot was moved close to the new train station near Alta Vista.

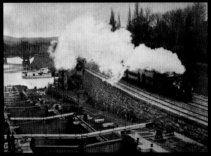

A steam locomotive, pulling a passenger train out of Québec, puffs its way slowly along the double tracks beside the Chateau Laurier, as it approaches Union Station. Trains, having crossed the Alexandra Bridge, could enter the station via a tunnel beneath Plaza Bridge and could, if they wished, continue out of the train shed south.

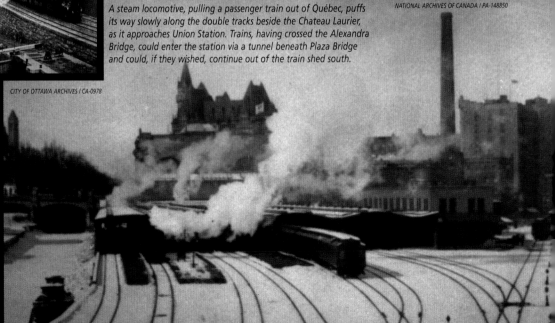

Once the terminus of commercial canal shipping and railway lines, the east side of the canal, south of Union Station, has changed greatly. The tracks disappeared in the sixties and were replaced by the scenic, and appropriately named, Colonel By Drive, which takes us north to the old station, now used as a government conference centre. Since the late 1960s, several modern buildings, including the National Arts Centre (left) and the Weston Hotel (right), have been added.

What a difference a few months can make. The failing light of a January afternoon reminds us all that Ottawa is truly a northern capital city. Throughout the bleakest days in the dead of winter, folks keep to their cars or bury themselves in warm clothing, but the beauty of this special spot is still here for those who will take the time to come out of their shells.

The Rideau Queen, a canal steamer, comes to the end of her voyage along the waterway. In 1896, there was still very little development in the area, but rail lines had now reached the spot where the proposed Union Station would be built. In the days before airliners, intercity buses and freeway travel, the railway penetrated to the very heart of big cities in order to deliver passengers close to their destination. The disruptive rail beds could cut a city in half and use up valuable real estate. As the city grew, and the canal's urban park potential was realized, this exquisite piece of real estate would catch the eye of civic planners.

Two canal barges lie in cribs for the winter of 1896. The canal and the locks throughout the system are drained every year to prevent expanding ice from crushing the stone and concrete walls. What is truly amazing about this photo however is what we don't see. Looking north from what is now the site of the National Arts Centre, we see a wooded field in the distance. This is Major's Hill and the site today of one of Ottawa's most beautiful parks. Between the viewer and the park these days lies the Chateau Laurier Hotel. The hotel would be completed in 1911 along with the stately Union Station, which now stands at right, where the buildings are in this shot.

At the turn of the century, there were several elegant pavilions along the canal, including Patterson Creek, Dow's Lake and this shingle-style boathouse near Lansdowne Park. The citizenry of Ottawa, dressed in their finest, enjoyed outings on the water and loved to gather for big events such as Regatta Day in 1909. Here Ottawans in canoes, rowboats, steam driven runabouts and punts of all descriptions make joyful use of a waterway designed for commerce and military deployment.
The grand veranda is lined with onlookers and you can almost hear the shouts of encouragement, the snap of flags, the splash of oars and the hoot of steam whistles.

Today, almost the entire length of the canal from Wellington Street to the Hog's Back Falls is lined in stone or concrete. The west side, from Dow's Lake to Hog's Back, however, is still rustic and natural like a riverbank. For many decades, most of the canal appeared as a slow moving river with trees and vegetation right down to the water's edge. In this shot taken at the end of the 19th century, day-tripping canoeists stop to chat with the owner of a small sailboat. The rising ground in the background, the narrow width and the gentle curve of the canal identify this bucolic spot as the stretch between Bank Street Bridge and Dunbar Bridge at Bronson Avenue.

One Man's Pain, Other Men's Pleasure

A GREAT MAN'S REPUTATION WAS SACRIFICED, ALONG WITH EXTENDED NAVIGATION ON THE OTTAWA RIVER, DUE IN PART TO THE VETO OF LEBRETON FLATS AS THE LOCATION FOR THE NORTHERN TERMINUS OF THE RIDEAU CANAL.

The British Government crushed Colonel By with trumped-up charges of cost overrun on the canal, a massive construction and engineering triumph of his own design hacked out of the untracked, malaria-rife wilderness between Ottawa and Kingston by the picks and shovels of unskilled labourers, its 24 dams and 45 locks conveying vessels up and down almost three times the height of Niagara Falls on their 202-kilometre (126-mile) journey. The 788,285 pounds sterling cost would have been somewhat less, however, had By been able to take the canal along the shortest, easiest route between Dow's Lake and the Ottawa River, that is, through Captain Le Breton's land.

Instead, By was forced to carve a tortuous channel that twisted its way northeast for eight kilometres (five miles) from Dow's Lake before ending in a 24-metre (80-foot) drop that compelled the construction of a steep flight of eight locks in order to provide staged access to the Ottawa River. By contrast, the route through Le Breton's property would have been only one-quarter the length, a short saunter straight north from the lake with easy access to the river at LeBreton Flats where, as a bonus, a lock or two could have skirted the Chaudière rapids and extended navigation further up the river.

However, Colonel By would take great comfort today in the knowledge that his town has benefited greatly from his misfortune. Every year, that "tortuous channel" lures tourists by the million. In summer, their pleasure craft ply its picturesque waters, navigating North America's oldest operating canal and berthing within the shadow of Canada's Parliament Buildings. In winter, they blissfully glide along its frozen extent, attracted by the fun and fame of the longest skating rink in the world.

Exactly ninety years later, the Victorian boathouse at Fifth Avenue and Queen Elizabeth Driveway has long since disappeared. For many years, this spot remained empty until, in the 1980s, it was replaced by a much smaller pavilion which houses a trendy yet friendly restaurant called the Canal Ritz. The canal at this point is quite wide and it still attracts lots of water activity in the summer and thousands of skating enthusiasts in the winter.

Brightly coloured umbrellas, people of every shape and size and spectacular gardens entice many diners, joggers, cyclists, strollers and boaters to the stretch of canal that skirts beautiful urban neighbourhoods such as the Golden Triangle and the Glebe.

In The Beginning

THE SACRED AND THE PROFANE SHARE EQUAL BILLING IN THE FOUNDING TWO CENTURIES AGO OF **OTTAWA,** CAPITAL CITY OF THE COUNTRY THAT GENERATES THE HIGHEST QUALITY OF LIFE IN THE WORLD, AS DETERMINED BY THE **UNITED NATIONS** AT THE THRESHOLD OF THE SECOND MILLENNIUM.

The city's location was decided by the sacred waters that flow in the ancient and mighty Ottawa River, that race over the seven cataracts of the mystic Chaudière Falls, and that course through the engineering marvel that became the Rideau Canal. The city's destiny, however, was impelled by the profane jealousy that existed between other communities with burning ambitions to lead the fledgling nation of Canada.

The 300-foot gothic height of the Peace Tower is framed by the entrance portico of the East Block. The Parliament Buildings house the Senate, Commons, Library and offices of Members of Parliament, Senators and their staffs.

THE PROFANE

CANADA'S SEAT OF GOVERNMENT FLIP-FLOPPED BETWEEN RIVAL CITIES KINGSTON, MONTREAL, QUEBEC CITY AND TORONTO, UNTIL QUEEN VICTORIA WAS ASKED TO PUT A STOP TO THIS 16-YEAR ADMINISTRATIVE NIGHTMARE.

In 1857, the Governor General of Canada advised Her Majesty that each of the pretenders was "jealous of every other city except Ottawa. The second vote of every place – save, perhaps, Toronto – would be given for Ottawa." And the rest is history. Except it almost wasn't, for in July 1858 the Parliament of Canada voted 64 to 50 against Victoria's choice.

It wasn't until some 18 months later that the parliamentarians changed their minds and adopted Ottawa as the capital of the Province of Canada and then, in 1867, of the expanding Dominion of Canada. A haughty Oxford University don retorted that the new capital was "a sub-arctic lumber village converted by royal mandate into a political cock-pit," while the US press praised the selection, declaring the new seat of government invincible to foreign invaders who would "inevitably be lost in the woods trying to find it."

And so Voltaire's "few acres of snow" which, 100 years earlier, the British government had debated trading in for the sun-soaked, sugar-, rum- and banana-rich islands of Guadeloupe, finally had a permanent capital.

For nearly a century, the silhouette of the Parliament Buildings and the swirling Ottawa River far below have made for the most spectacular of sunrises. Yet only a small number of Ottawans have ever witnessed these misty, marmalade skies, heard the cries of the wheeling seagulls or watched as the sun rose to warm the sandstone walls of Canada's greatest treasure. Every citizen should, at least once in a lifetime, set the alarm and take a stroll along Portage Bridge to take in the sight which remains privy only to intrepid photographers and insomniac joggers.

PARLIAMENT HILL
THE HEART OF THE CITY, THE HEART OF A NATION

In 1865, two years prior to Confederation, workers struggle to complete the Centre Block of the grand project. Considering the vast emptiness of the land, the still untested federation and the sparse population of what was to become the Dominion of Canada, the grandeur of the buildings is true testament to the expectations our forefathers had for this land.

From atop the mason's scaffold on the Centre Block, we gaze over the East Block under construction. In the far distance, we see only fields, barns, wagon tracks and a church. Without all the visual competition of a modern city, the new copper-roofed, sandstone structures must have projected an almost surreal aura in the Canadian wilderness.

The architects, supervisors and draughtsmen who designed and built our national treasure stand proudly for a formal photograph. Their patience, attention to detail and craftsmanship will last for generations to come.

The commanding site of Canada's Parliament Buildings, once surrounded by industry, is now the centrepiece for a national dream. Visitors to the top of the Peace Tower can look out to view the curvelinear forms of the Canadian Museum of Civilization and at right the National Gallery of Canada, the Canadian War Museum and the Royal Canadian Mint along Sussex Drive.

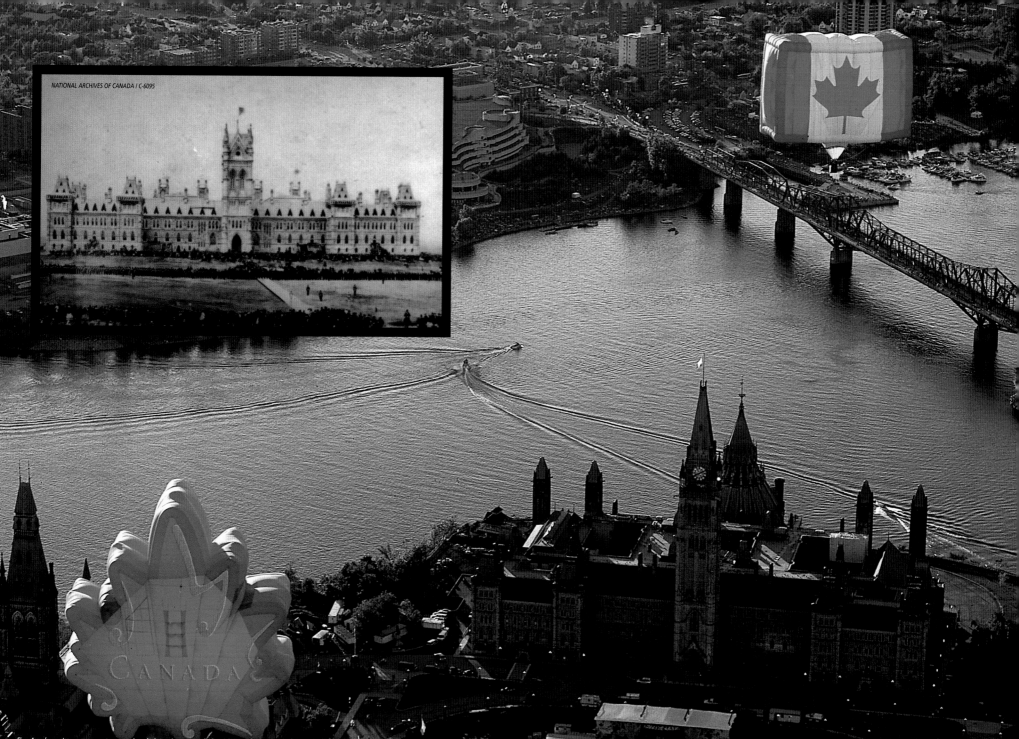

And we've never stopped celebrating. Back in 1867, the year of Confederation, there was so much to celebrate. A new and great country was stepping on to the world stage. The fresh sandstone edifices of the Dominion's new government were almost complete and it was Queen Victoria's birthday. Thousands crowd the lawns of Parliament (inset) to watch the military spectacle and share in one of our greatest moments. 131 years later, Canadians are still drawn by the thousands to where it all began. In 1867, July 1ˢᵗ (Dominion Day) was selected as our new National holiday and since then, Canada Day (as it became known in 1982) has become the greatest

National Capital Commission

AN EXPLOSIVE TRADITION THAT DIDN'T FIZZLE

CANADA DAY WITHOUT FIREWORKS IS UNTHINKABLE, LIKE A BIRTHDAY WITHOUT CAKE. HOWEVER, THIS SPECTACULAR TRADITION ALMOST DIDN'T GET OFF THE GROUND IN THE NATIONAL CAPITAL.

The 1867 Ottawa City Council declared July 1ˢᵗ a public holiday to mark the union of the provinces of Nova Scotia, New Brunswick, Quebec and Ontario in the Dominion of Canada. A committee was created "to arrange for the proper inauguration" of the new confederation but a persistent minority of councillors tried to cancel the celebration or, more specifically, the $500 set aside to pay for it. The nay sayers almost had their way, failing at times by only one single vote.

But fail they did and, with the exception of war years, dazzling pyrotechnic displays have been a hallmark of national birthday celebrations in the capital every July 1ˢᵗ ever since.

There are many wonderful vantagepoints around Entrance Bay from which to view the spectacular Canada Day fireworks display, but none are better that the lawns of Parliament Hill. Designed to be enjoyed from the Hill, the fireworks are a twenty-minute cannonade of colour, concussion and smoke. For the thousands of Canadians and tourists who crowd the Hill for the best view, there is also the ringing chorus of Ooohs and Ahhhs to provide the syncopation.

Until recently, the Peace Tower was centre stage for fireworks displays twice a year. In addition to the Canada Day show, another display happened annually at midnight on New Year's Eve. Despite the biting cold and late hour, the Hill was still crowded with spectators, tribute to the joy Ottawans found in their capital and in their winter.

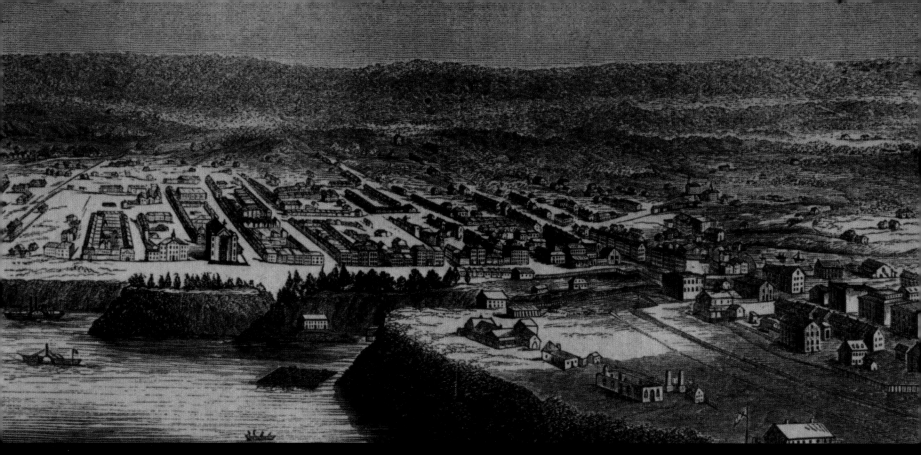

It took a creative mind to capture the newly chosen capital city from the air fifty years before the dawn of flight. In this etching looking due east, we see the bluffs of Parliament Hill, called Barracks Hill at the time, which was home to the British soldiers who were tasked with the construction of the canal system. The artist's over-eager mind's eye has conjured a mountain range east of town which has yet to be discovered.

SHIPS, RESERVOIRS AND LUNATICS ON PARLIAMENT HILL

DOCKS LARGER THAN THOSE IN LONDON, ENGLAND AND A HARBOUR THAT REQUIRED WATER TO RUN UPHILL WERE ONCE DESTINED FOR WHAT TODAY IS OTTAWA'S PARLIAMENTARY PRECINCT.

Lieutenant-Colonel John By – the brilliant Royal Engineer who remains the city's most significant and yet least known historical figure – was so committed to this concept that he illegitimately expropriated 32 hectares (80 acres) of land for the purpose. He also planned fortifications around Parliament Hill similar to those at Quebec City on which he had worked earlier in the century. However, as he turned British blueprints for the new community at the northern terminus of the Rideau Canal into reality between 1826 and 1832, these projects were ultimately unrealized.

Some 30 years later, the majestic bluffs that today boast Canada's Houses of Parliament were earmarked for a reservoir. The two wells that had serviced the community since the early 1840s were proving to be inadequate for an expanding population and so a gravity-fed water and sewage system was designed by Thomas Coltrin Keefer, one of only two Canadians to be elected president of the American Society of Civil Engineers

140 years later, we see that one of the most beautiful cities in the world has risen from the site of old Bytown – fanning out south, east and west of By's locks, devouring former outlying towns and villages. With the aid of a flying machine, we need not imagine it in our mind's eye anymore. Even the most creative mind could not have fantasized such a rich and shining jewel of a city.

The plan was eagerly embraced by City Council, however the provincial government quickly squashed the idea.

The destiny of the primeval beech ridge that had once housed the garrison of Colonel By's Royal Engineers was finally fulfilled the following year. On September 1st, 1860, the cornerstone of the Legislature of Canada was laid by Queen Victoria's 19-year-old son, the future King Edward VII. As construction of the imposing buildings proceeded, they elicited remarkable responses including that of *The Times of London* correspondent N.A. Woods, who sneered: "(The buildings are) admirably suited for lunatic asylums, whenever the town is sufficiently prosperous to require them for that purpose."

Ultimately, however, Woods proclaimed the modern Gothic structures to be the "finest… in all America." And for the next 100 years, the Centre Block and the two departmental buildings dominated the city, not least on the days when half-burnt two-dollar bills rained on the parliamentary lawn, escapees from the chimney of the faulty East Block furnace used until 1938 to incinerate worn Bank of Canada bills.

A Knight On
A White River

SIR GALAHAD PERFORMED HIS FINAL ACT OF CHIVALRY IN OTTAWA, OR SO WILLIAM LYON MACKENZIE KING – WHO LATER WAS TO LEAD CANADA THROUGH THE SECOND WORLD WAR – WOULD HAVE HAD US BELIEVE.

On December 6th, 1901, Henry Harper, a senior official in the Department of Labour, drowned in a futile attempt to rescue Bessie Blair, daughter of the Minister of Railways and Canals, while skating on the early winter ice of the Ottawa River. To immortalize his friend's heroism, King erected a statue of the most gallant of King Arthur's knights on Wellington Street in front of the nation's Houses of Parliament.

It is a sure bet that the tragic drownings did not occur on a Sunday. For much of the early 20th century, skating on the river on Sundays was forbidden by law.

A lone Ottawan ventures across the great frozen basin known as Entrance Bay. In the depth of winter's freeze, this is a non-recommended but awe-inspiring vantagepoint from which to view our capital. In the early winter and spring however, the deceptive ice can be a lethal environment, as Bessie Blair learned in 1901.

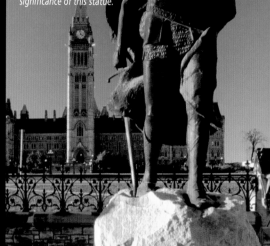

Sir Galahad stands for all to see on Wellington Street, but very few Ottawans know and appreciate the significance of this statue.

Queen Victoria's icy stare seems all the colder for her early winter coat of freezing rain.

Queen Elizabeth II, a great horsewoman, is depicted astride a charger.

From atop his granite pedestal on the east lawn, Sir Wilfred Laurier, the seventh Prime Minister of Canada, gazes at his namesake, the Chateau Laurier Hotel. From this well-deserved place, Laurier can see every sunrise and watch the growth of this great city.

As in any seat of government anywhere in the world, there are a number of statues that grace the lawns around Parliament Hill. They pay tribute to Royalty and to the greatest statesmen in the history of this country. During the first 132 years, we have been governed by only twenty Prime Ministers. Some made incalculable contributions to shape our history; some were gone in a flash. Of those who have long since passed away, the greatest are honoured in bronze and granite.

The placement of these two former Prime Ministers, legendary political antagonists, is interesting. John Diefenbaker stands alone near the West Block and, while he has a fine view of the front of the Hill, Lester Pearson has a better view, a comfortable chair and Queen Victoria for company. And Mr. Pearson is also in a position to stare at his rival's back for all eternity.

John George Diefenbaker, the 13th Prime Minister and the first from Western Canada.

Lester Bowles Pearson was Canada's 14th Prime Minister and a world statesman. As Canada's ambassador to the United Nations, he created the UN peacekeeping force and won the Nobel Prize for Peace. His lasting Canadian legacy however, will surely be the creation of the Canadian flag.

Thomas D'Arcy McGee, an Irish-born poet and orator, was one of the Fathers of Confederation. He was shot dead on Sparks Street in 1868 by a Fenian radical for denouncing their violent tactics.

Sir George Etienne-Cartier was one of eight Fathers of Confederation from the "Province of Canada" (Upper and Lower) who, along with 15 other "Fathers", created what was to become Canada.

Scottish-born Alexander Mackenzie, the second Prime Minister of Canada and a stonemason by trade, defeated Sir John A. MacDonald over a scandal involving the building of the Canadian Pacific Railway.

Sir Robert Borden, Canada's eighth and the first Canadian-born Prime Minister, governed the nation during the First World War.

William Lyon Mackenzie King, one of Canada's truly eccentric characters and our tenth Prime Minister, led Canada throughout the Second World War.

t appears that the only remaining bell from the original Centre Block tower, which crashed through the burning Victoria Tower to the ground after ringing out the final stroke of midnight on February 3rd, 1916, has been suspended above the new Victory Tower during construction. As supervisors look on, workers take turns striking the bell with their sledges. Eighty years later, we ponder on the reason why it was hoisted to the top for all to hear one last time. For years, this very bell sat silent on a granite slab behind the Parliamentary Library for all to view and touch.

ohn George Diefenbaker, the charismatic and firebrand Prime Minister, warms his stern and bronze countenance in the sunshine of a perfect summer day. As the first Prime Minister from Canada's West (Saskatchewan), "Dief the Chief" was granted a prime spot on the western end of the Center Block.

The Parliament Buildings, and the lawns that they surround, are icons of Canada's federal system and Ottawa's place in the Nation's history. On these lawns, we come together to celebrate, to mourn, to protest, to watch, to be heard and to share our heritage. This special open space has seen traditions and spectacle, peace and anger as well as frisbees and placards.

PEACE TOWER

TIME STANDS STILL, TIME RINGS OUT

Throughout the seasons, the Peace Tower stands resolute and elegant – breathtaking yet understated, massive yet fascinating in its detail.

Like all things Canadian, the Center Block and the Peace Tower come alive with winter. Each December, the National Capital Commission decks the trees and bushes around Parliament Hill with many thousands of coloured lights. Purples, reds, blues, greens and yellows of every description are worked together into a symphony of riotous colour. Crews work feverishly for weeks in sub-zero weather and, a fortnight before Christmas, thousands of Ottawans flock to the Hill for the throwing of the switch. At the appointed hour, the lights are turned on and the ooohs! and ahhhs! can be heard across the country. In an instant, the darkened grounds of the Hill are transformed - much to the delight of children of all ages.

Though not many know it, the sculpting of stone on Parliament Hill is ongoing to this day. Inside and out, the arches, columns, windows and walls of the three main buildings are adorned with literally hundreds of sculpted animals, mythological beasts, coats of arms and gargoyles. It seems as if no two are the same and the work is endless as stone sculptors continue to chip away at the blocks of sandstone.

Ottawa is the capital city of a great northern country. We wear winter well. Here the ice-coated trees of Major's Hill Park sparkle in the bright midday sun. Across the locks from the park, and to the west, lies Parliament Hill and the snow-covered spires of the Centre Block and the Library. The true beauty of this architectural wonder is that it is breathtaking from every angle and from every vantagepoint. When architects were contemplating its design, they knew full well that the high site would afford views from all directions and they rose to the challenge.

The tension and fear in the minds of Ottawa's citizens is almost palpable, as they stand on the west side of Parliament Hill to watch the progress of the Great Fire of 1900. There was absolutely no guarantee that the fire, which had already swept through Hull and Lebreton Flats, would not totally engulf their precious city. One did not have to be on Parliament Hill to fully grasp the immensity of the firestorm, for smoke was visible throughout much of Eastern Ontario and at night the orange glow of the fire could be seen as far away as Brockville and Kingston.

Ottawans take what they can carry and flee from the raging hell which consumes their homes. As flames approach the west end of Queen Street near the escarpment, terrified citizens are paralyzed with fear and the chaos is evident. One can almost hear the shouts, the sobs, the whinnies of spooked horses, the clatter of metal-clad wheels on stone and the distant roar of the flames. The fashionable area of Ottawa consumed by the fire never recovered from the devastation. Homeowners, fearing another fire fed by the nearby lumberyards, simply relocated to other areas such as Sandy Hill or south to Centre Town.

FIRE

THE THREAT OF FIRE IS NEVER FAR AWAY, WHEN A CITY IS SURROUNDED BY FOREST.

In August 1870, up-stream forest fires ravaged both sides of the Ottawa River. As flames threatened the west end of the town, quick thinkers broke the dam on the north side of Dow's Lake, allowing water to pour straight north down Preston Street to the Ottawa River, forming an effective moat barrier.

Two years later, approval was finally given for the construction near LeBreton Flats of a waterworks system which could deliver 45,000,000 litres (10,000,000 gallons) of untreated water every 24 hours. This was followed by the decision to maintain a salaried fire department whose members were on duty 24-hours a day, seven days a week, living with their families in quarters over the fire station. It wasn't until 1919 that the platoon system was adopted, allowing men to work in shifts. And it was a further two years before Ontario law said they must have one day off a week.

The Great Fire of Ottawa-Hull started in Hull on April 26th, 1900 and changed the face of both communities forever. Before it ended, it had claimed seven lives and left thousands homeless. Fed by piles of lumber along the river banks, flames crossed the river at the Chaudière and devoured lumber mills (including most of the lifework of an uninsured E.B. Eddy), flour mills, electric generating stations and hundreds of homes, among them those of the rich and influential who, until then, had favoured that area of the capital. At sundown, a decrease in the westerly wind fortuitously combined with the high escarpment at Bronson Avenue to stop the flames from reaching into the downtown core. The Chaudière area was eventually rebuilt, but this time with dwellings for low-income mill workers and, today, even those have disappeared.

On the bitter cold night of February 3rd, 1916, an inferno blazes from the windows of the dying Centre Block. The silhouette of the Victoria Tower is partially obscured by heavy smoke and steam, as firefighters with limited manpower and equipment, fight a losing battle. At midnight, the automatic bells of the tower rang out one last and ghostly time, then, in a shower of sparks, crashed down though the burning timbers and were silenced for all time.

The stone and concrete Parliament Buildings were believed to be fireproof and so were constructed without even one fire escape and equipped with very little firefighting equipment. However, on the bitter cold night of February 3rd, 1916, flames gutted the Centre Block, claiming the lives of seven people and destroying the House of Commons and the Senate, sparing only the Parliamentary Library. As the conflagration raced towards the Senate Chamber, staff managed to remove several priceless paintings including a portrait of Queen Victoria by the English artist John Partridge. In 1849, this same painting had been rescued by parliamentary assistant librarian Alpheus Todd from a purposefully-set fire in the Parliament Buildings in Montreal. Sixty-seven years later, the person responsible for saving it again was Mr. Todd's nephew, Hamlyn Todd.

The morning of February, 4th 1916 revealed the full extent of the damage. The Centre Block itself was damaged beyond salvage, but the cathedral-like Parliamentary Library remained. An Ottawa Fire Department pumper truck stands watch on the north side of Parliament Hill, making sure that the Library stays untouched by flame. It would be a full ten years before the completion of a new Centre Block and Tower, but this would be an even more beautiful design

Your Money Or Your Sweat

Until 1850, all Ottawa men between 21 and 60 years of age were compelled to work on road repair and maintenance for two to 27 days a year, according to the value of the property they owned in the city. They also had to keep the sidewalk in front of their property free of snow, creating difficulties for pedestrians when some cleared in the morning and others at night.

This statute labour method of city maintenance was commuted in 1850 to the payment of 65 cents per day of work due – the start of property tax rates. The city assessor determined the value of every property for the purpose of this taxation, killing two birds with one stone by also inquiring about the income of every resident for federal purposes after income tax was introduced in 1917 to help the war effort.

In spite of the security of property tax income, executions against the corporation once cost the city the impoundment of its fire engines. Even the chairs in the council chambers, "the very chairs upon which aldermen were sitting," were under seizure for debt at one time. This was because City Council was required to meet its expenditures every year and so any unforeseen expenses could cripple the corporation.

In 1860, the city planned for and purchased two 1053 kilogram (2340 pound) hook-and-ladder carts for the fire department. Unfortunately, they did not budget for a team of horses to pull them. Consequently, the carts had to be drawn by a squad of 20 men.

Such complications were taken in stride in a town which had discovered in 1849, fully two years after incorporation, that Queen Victoria had vetoed its legal status, thus rendering all acts of the mayor and council over the past two years invalid. This situation was remedied on January 1st, 1850 when Bytown was finally confirmed a town.

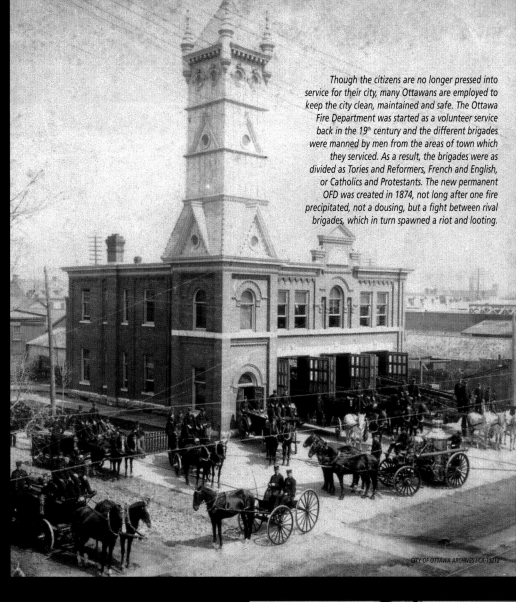

Though the citizens are no longer pressed into service for their city, many Ottawans are employed to keep the city clean, maintained and safe. The Ottawa Fire Department was started as a volunteer service back in the 19th century and the different brigades were manned by men from the areas of town which they serviced. As a result, the brigades were as divided as Tories and Reformers, French and English, or Catholics and Protestants. The new permanent OFD was created in 1874, not long after one fire precipitated, not a dousing, but a fight between rival brigades, which in turn spawned a riot and looting.

CITY OF OTTAWA ARCHIVES / CA-15212

In 1899, members of the Ottawa Fire Department pose with their modern ladder and pumper equipment. The high, elegant tower was used for drying hoses after a fire.

CITY OF OTTAWA ARCHIVES / CA-3491

Three members of the new Ottawa Fire Department strike an heroic pose in front of Fire Station N°. 2 at Lyon and Queen Streets. Though operated by determined firemen, the equipment was largely ineffectual and fire – the great renewer – continued to plague the city.

In 1954, the OFD had come a long way in the eighty years since the first brigades of municipal firefighters were hired. Old N°.2 Station, from the previous page, is now a full-sized, modern firehall with pumpers and a ladder truck.

Throughout the past couple of decades, Ottawa and the surrounding municipalities have undergone a firehall rebuilding program. The old facilities could not handle the advanced technologies and sizes of today's equipment, and so were scheduled to be replaced. Some of the old fire halls were built on land too small to take a new facility, so the halls were relocated. Some of the elegant and historic old halls (such as the ones on Sunnyside Avenue and Parkdale Avenue) were handed over to the city for use as community centres.

By 1927, the equipment was getting more powerful and the men better trained. The sharply dressed firefighters of Fire Station N°.7 on Somerset Street, strike a fearless pose with their new pumper truck.

The ultimate embarrassment for firefighters is to have to put up with the comments and jokes, as they try to extinguish a fully involved fire at one of their own firehalls. In 1948, neighbouring units of old Station N°.1 on Duke Street struggle to put out the blaze on a winter's day.

Today, Fire Station N°.1 is a modern building, which is much better designed to avoid destruction by fire.

POLICE DEPARTMENT
LAW AND ORDER OF THE DAY

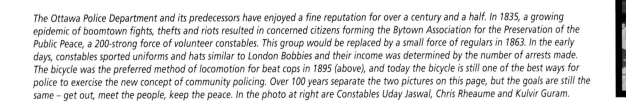

CITY OF OTTAWA ARCHIVES / CA-1216

The Ottawa Police Department and its predecessors have enjoyed a fine reputation for over a century and a half. In 1835, a growing epidemic of boomtown fights, thefts and riots resulted in concerned citizens forming the Bytown Association for the Preservation of the Public Peace, a 200-strong force of volunteer constables. This group would be replaced by a small force of regulars in 1863. In the early days, constables sported uniforms and hats similar to London Bobbies and their income was determined by the number of arrests made. The bicycle was the preferred method of locomotion for beat cops in 1895 (above), and today the bicycle is still one of the best ways for police to exercise the new concept of community policing. Over 100 years separate the two pictures on this page, but the goals are still the same – get out, meet the people, keep the peace. In the photo at right are Constables Uday Jaswal, Chris Rheaume and Kulvir Guram.

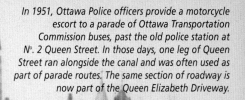

In 1951, Ottawa Police officers provide a motorcycle escort to a parade of Ottawa Transportation Commission buses, past the old police station at Nº. 2 Queen Street. In those days, one leg of Queen Street ran alongside the canal and was often used as part of parade routes. The same section of roadway is now part of the Queen Elizabeth Driveway.

The ultimate expression of the policeman has always been the motorcycle cop. Today, Ottawa operates a small contingent of highly mobile motorcycle cops for traffic and escort duties. When a visiting head of state needs the route from the airport to Rideau Hall cleared, these units are the van. The first OPD Motorcycle Squad (top) was constituted in 191 with regular bikes as well as sidecar units. In 1950 (center), the rides were more powerful but the duty still prestigious. Constables Chaughan Garve and Amerjit Sahota, known as Traffic Services Officers, are now part of a giant Regional Police force which was formed by the amalgamation of the municipal police forces of the region.

CHANGING THE GUARD

STANDING GUARD OVER TRADITION

Shining brass, gold braid, scarlet tunic and immaculate leather. In an age of high-tech soldiering and electronic entertainment, the traditional uniforms, precise drill and stirring martial music of the Ceremonial Guard still raise goosebumps on the most jaded youth. Thousands of onlookers line the perimeter of the east lawn each day to view the spectacle. The 135 soldiers and band members begin their daily march at the Cartier Square Drill Hall along the Rideau Canal. From this armoury, they advance west along Laurier Avenue, wheeling onto Elgin. The rousing pipes and brass and the crunch of boots can be heard above the din of the city and many tourists rush from their hotels and adjoining streets to join them, as they move out for Parliament Hill.

Awe-struck boys and girls of all ages are mesmerized by the scarlet troop and, as it passes, they fall-in like the children of Hamlin. Inevitably, smiles beam from everyone as one or two brave little soldiers get caught up in the sight, sticking out their chests while marching along with the Guard. At last, with pipes skirling and trumpets blaring, they swing on to Wellington Street, past the waiting crowds and through the gate to the lawns of Parliament Hill.

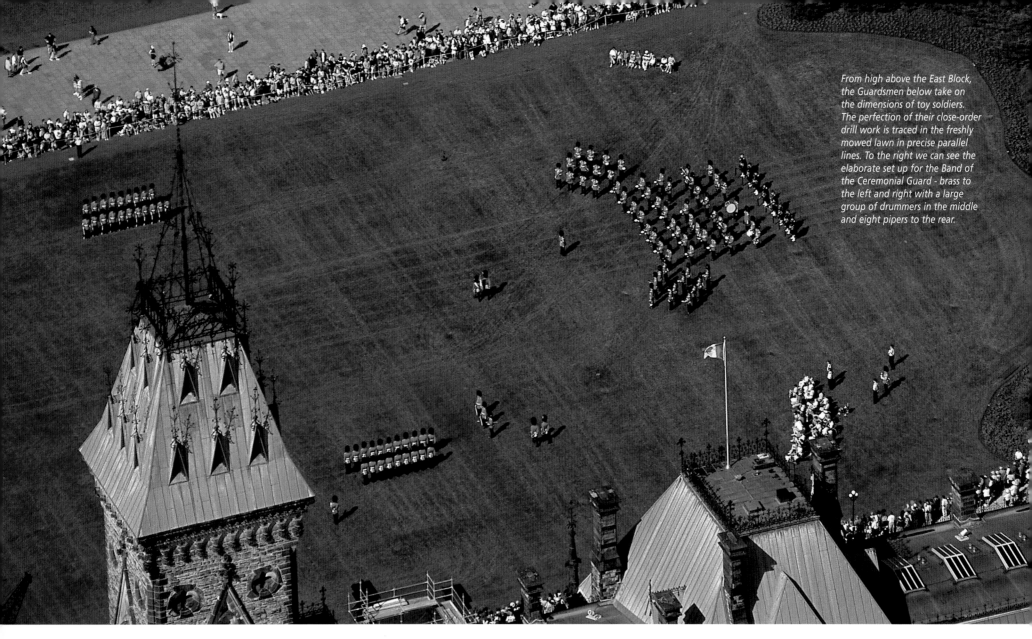

From high above the East Block, the Guardsmen below take on the dimensions of toy soldiers. The perfection of their close-order drill work is traced in the freshly mowed lawn in precise parallel lines. To the right we can see the elaborate set up for the Band of the Ceremonial Guard - brass to the left and right with a large group of drummers in the middle and eight pipers to the rear.

Second only to the image of the Peace Tower itself, the bearskin cap-wearing Guardsman is an often-used symbol of the Nation's Capital.

Since 1979, the faces of women could be seen amongst the faces of the Guardsmen.

The uniforms of the Canadian Grenadier Guards of the Ceremonial Guard trace their roots to the Grenadier Guards of Great Britain. The enormous black bearskin caps, as you would think, can be unbearably hot. Traditional red tunics are trimmed with white brass buttons and brocaded emblems in the form of a 'grenade fired proper'.

When the temperatures of summer soar to 30 degrees and above, the Guardsmen do not wear a lighter uniform. Years ago, in one of the greatest and toughest of military traditions, soldiers who were overcome with heat, were expected to pass out standing to attention. Every once in a while, a pale and wavering Guardsman, who had forgotten to eat a good breakfast, would fall face first into the freshly mowed grass and would stay there, face down, until he recovered. These days, being gentler times, the fallen soldiers are attended to right away, but they are still expected to fall well.

On Parliament Hill, both the Mounties and the Guardsmen do double duty posing with delighted tourists. At the left, a medal-bedecked member of the Governor General's Foot Guards gives a family of tourists a momento to remember.

The Ceremonial Guard is made even more spectacular by the stirring sounds of kilted pipers.

A Mountie in modern dress and one in the uniform of the original Northwest Mounted Police pose with their chargers on the shady lawn in front of Rideau Hall.

In celebration of the 125th anniversary of the RCMP, Mounties dress in vintage Northwest Mounted Police uniforms to the delight of children and adults.

Tourists and citizens alike can enjoy the occasional open-air concert by the Band of The Ceremonial Guard.

RIDEAU HALL
A COLONIAL PAST, A ROYAL ATTRACTION

Rideau Hall is not only an important part of Ottawa's heritage, but of Canada's as well. It is primarily the residence of the Governor General, the Queen's representative in Canada. At the outset, these Royal appointees were traditionally aristocrats from Great Britain, but since the days of Vincent Massey, they have been chosen from the ranks of accomplished and diplomatic Canadians. Rideau Hall is where all foreign ambassadors must present their Letters of Credence and where visiting heads of state are put up during their stay in the Nation's Capital. Grounds keepers take advantage, on some occasions, to have the dignitary plant a new tree on the lawn in front of the main entrance. A brief stroll through the trees will reveal plaques with the names of some of the world's most influential statesmen and figures - names like John F. Kennedy, Nelson Mandela, Dwight D. Eisenhower, Diana, Princess of Wales and Margaret Thatcher.

Originally constructed in 1838 by Thomas MacKay, a wealthy stonemason and contractor, the structure graced what was known then as "MacKay's Bush". The house, nicknamed "MacKay's Castle" was considered remote from the rest of Bytown, connected by little more than a path, but was chosen for its modern luxuries such as central heating and running water. Such was the state of the road that the first Governor General actually boarded a Royal Navy cutter at Governor's Bay on the river, below what is now the Prime Minister's Residence. He was then rowed the short distance to the Ottawa Locks, where a carriage awaited.

The name "Rideau Hall" is reported to have been suggested by MacKay's daughter Elizabeth in honour of the work he completed on the Rideau Canal and for his mills at Rideau Falls. Almost the entire structure of the original residence (inset) is hidden by a series of additions, which have been constructed since the initial purchase.

Since the earliest days, the game of cricket has been played on the pitch to the south of the Rideau Hall. While few play the game today, Canadians whose heritage is rooted in such countries as Jamaica, Australia, Pakistan or India, continue to enjoy a few innings of the gentleman's game.

Viscount Monck, the first Governor General of the Dominion of Canada, presided over the 1867 ceremonies which brought Canada into existence. His family poses on the south lawn of the newly upgraded vice-regal residence.

The modern-day residence is a showpiece of elegance and hospitality. Each year, the Governor General's New Year's Eve Levee, as well as a spectacular Garden Party open to all Canadians and hosted by the Governor General, takes place in the immaculately maintained gardens of Rideau Hall (lower centre). This is the same location depicted in the historic photo above.

The original Main Gate and Lodge were added after Rideau Hall was purchased from Thomas MacKay. The Queen's Representative, in a country not yet formed, was a very important figure, warranting a permanent, round-the-clock British Army guard. Later the role of Governor General became largely tradition, warranting police protection and only a ceremonial guard.

A piper leads three fresh Guardsmen of the Canadian Grenadier Guards out of the main gate of Rideau Hall to relieve the two who now stand to attention outside their posts. It is forbidden for sentries to talk to or acknowledge anyone, except in the line of duty. Just as in Great Britain, obnoxious tourists, attractive women and testy children will try to get a reaction from the sentries in many ways, but they must not, under any circumstances, react.

From high above the regal Main Gate of Rideau Hall, we see the Gate Lodge (top) which originally housed the relief and a permanent guard. As well, we see the sentry positions in front of the gate. The sentries alternate between standing to statue-like attention and patrolling in reflected unison along the royal blue, wooden platforms which extend from their guard posts. Busloads of tourists disembark for the obligatory photo posing with a stone-faced Guardsman. While the colourful guard occupies the tourists, the actual guard, a member of the The Corps of Commissionaires, keeps cool in the air-conditioned booth just visible behind the left gate post.

An aerial view of the Rideau Hall grounds at the peak of fall colour shows us just how stunning this Canadian treasure is. At the bottom we see the open space of the traditional cricket pitch and at lower right, the gardens which are the site of much gracious hospitality. Virtually all of the large orange, red and yellow coloured trees along and below the main drive were planted by the world's greatest dignitaries. You will find there the names of kings and queens, dukes and duchesses, presidents and prime ministers, warriors and peacemakers. It is a special space open to all Canadians, but only a few short years ago, it was suggested that the grounds be closed to the public for security reasons. The outcry from Canadians who felt that it belonged to ordinary citizens, as much as to the world's elite, convinced officials to keep the gate open. This is truly our national home.

Their Royal Highnesses, the Duke and Duchess of Cornwall and York, at a reception at Rideau Hall, 1901.

Governor General Vincent Massey, brother of 1940s and '50s film star Raymond Massey, relaxes in the garden with his granddaughters in 1957.

(Middle) After an 1891 cricket match on the grounds of Rideau Hall, members of the Ottawa Cricket Club pose in all their Britannic splendour.

(Far right) Sports have always been an important part of life at Rideau Hall. Governor General Lord Dufferin (namesake of Dufferin Bridge, standing with broom at left) enjoys a friendly game of curling in the 1870s.

Earnscliffe, the present day residence of the British High Commissioner, occupies one of the choicest building sites in all Ottawa. This pristine Gothic Revival house (above), built in 1855 for lumber baron John MacKinnon (a son-in-law of Thomas MacKay), stands on a high promontory which offers sweeping views up and down the Ottawa River. Fortune did not smile on MacKinnon and he died bankrupt in 1866. The house was picked up for a song by Thomas Keefer, another son-in-law of his more astute business partner Thomas MacKay. In 1871, the house was rented to Sir John A. Macdonald who eventually purchased it in 1883 and named it Earnscliffe. He lived here until his death in 1891, while still in office as Prime Minister. The sumptuous gardens are said to be the venue for some of Ottawa's most elegant and aristocratic soirées. Since 1930, the British Union Jack has waved resolutely from Earnscliffe's staff, while a few hundred metres away on the other side of Rideau Falls, the standard of Canada's other founding nation, flies equally proudly from France's Embassy.

While not nearly as elegant a structure as Earnscliffe, the imposing walls of Laurier House have seen their fair share of history. It was first built in 1878 for local jeweler John Leslie (the Leslie family and their nanny pose with their new home above) and was purchased by Prime Minister Wilfred Laurier in 1897, a year after he took office. Originally the address was on Thomas Street, but after Laurier's death in 1919, it was changed to Laurier Avenue. When Lady Laurier died in 1921, she bequeathed the home to another Liberal, party leader William Lyon MacKenzie King. He became Prime Minister within the year and named the residence Laurier House in honour of his predecessor. King, who was said to have communicated spiritually with his deceased mother while in the house, died there in 1950. It was given to him as a gift and in return, he gave it to the Canadian people. Today, it is a National Historic Monument and is beautifully restored and maintained by Parks Canada - a museum dedicated to its two esteemed occupants.

CASCADES
COURSING THROUGH TIME

Waterways have played an important role in the history and development of Ottawa. The Rideau River, Ottawa River, Gatineau River and Rideau Canal functioned as the commercial arteries of the region for centuries and, in terms of tourism, still do. The Rideau Canal, the undisputed key element in the historical, cultural and commercial growth of the city, would not have been built were it not for the fact that major sections of the Rideau River were totally and forever non-navigable. The locks were constructed at Entrance Bay simply because the Rideau River ended its gentle meandering journey through town by plummeting forty feet vertically. The next two sets of locks along the waterway (Hartwell's and Hog's Back) were also constructed to circumvent the thundering cascade at Hog's Back.

Rideau Falls and Hog's Back Falls have remained somewhat the same since the days when voyageurs and native hunters were forced to portage around them. Today they draw tourists, lovers and citizens who gaze upon the tumultuous waterfalls and shout above the din. Both have their own distinct qualities. Rideau Falls is a miniature Niagara, with two distinct curtains of brown Rideau River water slipping swiftly to their thundering deaths forty feet below. Hog's Back Falls (this page) is a wildly careening cacophony of crashing water, misting plumes, swirling eddies and multiple cascades. In springtime at the height of snow melt, these two waterfalls become swollen and turn into awe-inspiring if not frightening natural wonders.

While the Ottawa River does not go through such precipitous vertical changes, it has its own characteristic areas where the water picks up speed over a rocky bottom. The cascade known as Chaudière Falls surges to a pounding roar in springtime, though it remains controlled by dams throughout the much of the year. It was once considered one of the most magnificent natural spectacles in all of North America. Two centuries of wood cutting, dam building and mill construction have simply obliterated this once-thundering tumult by which all others in the region were judged. We can only envy such people as Champlain and Wright who saw the area before it was ever touched by axe or hammer.

In addition to Chaudière Falls, the Ottawa boasts the fast-moving waters known as Remic Rapids up-river near Champlain Bridge and those down-river from Britannia Bay which remain a playground for intrepid kayakers year round.

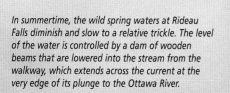

In summertime, the wild spring waters at Rideau Falls diminish and slow to a relative trickle. The level of the water is controlled by a dam of wooden beams that are lowered into the stream from the walkway, which extends across the current at the very edge of its plunge to the Ottawa River.

For those with an inclination to visit Rideau Falls, there is, aside from the noisy spectacle, the constant and spiritual interplay of water and light.

NATIONAL ARCHIVES OF CANADA / C-116463

CITY OF OTTAWA ARCHIVES / CA-15190

Where voyageurs saw impediment and good reason to rest for the night, the future Scottish lumber barons saw money. Falling water created kinetic energy. Kinetic energy powered saws. Saws milled logs into lumber. Lumber sold for money. Thomas MacKay, a stonemason and contractor, came to Bytown to help construct Colonel By's locks, but he knew a good thing when he saw one (excuse the pun). He wasted no time, purchasing the land around the falls and beginning his monopoly over the area, which saw him become a wealthy man and a key political player in the early history of Ottawa. In the early ink sketch above, lumbermen manoeuvre their log raft for a closer look at the falls.

Below, we see that the land around the waterfall was fully developed for milling by 1855, but still in a natural state with tall fir trees in abundance. The gentleman in the top hat and waistcoat (outdoor adventure wear in its day) takes in the sight from a rocky outcropping. Such antics today would bring on the fire department rescue team and a specially trained police negotiator.

In the photo above, taken in 1869, the MacKay milling operation is a going concern. Employing hundreds, the mills made Thomas MacKay a rich man. His concentration of commerce and the residential community of New Edinburgh, which he developed, soon rivaled Bytown and Wrightstown for dominance over the region. In this picture (as well as the two below) we see that there was a short shelf running squarely across the mouth of the falls 30 feet before the edge. While this four foot change in the level of the riverbed still exists today, it is obscured by a walkway and gateworks which cross the river directly above.

Rideau Falls is, like its big sister Niagara, actually two waterfalls separated by an island in the middle of the flow. The western and smaller of the two curtains is seen here in the depths of winter in 1874. The constant flow of water and wind driven mists have caked the mills with a thick coating of ice. These sawmills must have been horrendous places to work with shrieking saw blades, crashing timber, freezing temperatures and grievous industrial accidents.

NATIONAL ARCHIVES OF CANADA / PA-8347

On a bright but freezing winter day, the constantly moving water of the Rideau River slips silently from beneath its icy mantle to drop forty thundering feet from the limestone escarpment to the Ottawa River. Far below, the foaming and swirling current is swept mercilessly beneath the thick ice of the Ottawa, never to be seen again. It is a frightening sight indeed for the active imagination.

To avoid the crushing build-up of floating ice during the spring run-off, city maintenance crews blast and cut the ice for miles above the falls. The huge pieces float downstream from the work parties, picking up speed at the last second only to slip silently into space, crashing into the river below.

In summer the ice build-up melts away to a sparkling curtain of water, much to the delight of the passengers on the Paula D, an Ottawa River tour boat. In the days of its natural flowing state, long before the coming of the Scottish industrialists, Rideau Falls was a wild, voluminous and steady wall of water which inspired explorers to stop and write matching torrents of heady prose.

Green Island has not always been the focus of municipal democracy in action. Even 70 years ago, it was quite different from the gracious park and municipal centre that we know it as today. It was, instead, a mill site of enormous proportions. Here long ago, the first saw mills of Jean-Baptiste St. Louis and the distillery and lumber and grist mills of Thomas MacKay brought to Bytown tough and hardworking men. Below the falls, on the Ottawa River, the French raftsmen, who steered their giant rafts downstream, would come ashore to let off some steam. The result of the hard work and hard drinking was a rough and wild town, where a man was just as likely to fight you as befriend you. Violence and lawlessness came to a head during the Stony Monday Riots, which spurred citizens to regain control from the hooligan gangs.

FROM ANARCHY TO DEMOCRACY

OTTAWA WAS REPUTED TO BE THE MOST LAWLESS COMMUNITY IN BRITISH NORTH AMERICA IN THE MID-1830s, FROM WHOSE STREETS, IT WAS ONCE SAID, IT WAS HARDER TO ESCAPE UNSCATHED THAN FROM THE TERRORS OF A LION'S DEN. THE COMPLETION OF THE RIDEAU CANAL HAD LED TO THE TOTAL COLLAPSE OF EMPLOYMENT IN THE COMMUNITY, THEN KNOWN AS BYTOWN, AND ANARCHY ENSUED.

It is no surprise, then, that the corrupting influence of democracy on spiritual values was the subject of the first book believed printed in Bytown, published in 1837 by the unconventional minister of the community's first Anglican congregation. And the following year, American textbooks were banned from local schools because they touted democracy over monarchic institutions.

Voting in the "democracy" of 19th century Ottawa was equally dramatic. One by one, the owners of unmortgaged property in the city stepped onto a platform outside the voting poll and publicly proclaimed their name, address, occupation and their candidate of choice. As the spectacle progressed, supporters of losing candidates sometimes used brute force to prevent opposing electors from casting their vote or to speed up their own.

Things came to a head in the Stony Monday Riots of September 17th, 1849 with the total disintegration of a tension-filled meeting in the Byward Market of Tory and Reformist partisans – opposing sides on the question of whether to welcome or censure British North America's Governor-in-Chief, Lord Elgin, when he visited Bytown with an eye to moving the capital from Montreal. Sticks and stones flew thick in the air, firearms were quickly procured from nearby stores, 30 people were injured and one person killed before a garrison company arrived to put an end to the fighting. For the time being.

The following Wednesday, Tories in Upper Town, west of the canal, prepared for a second meeting by mustering 1,700 men, nine pieces of cannon and 1,000 stand of small arms. They were matched in Lower Town, east of the canal, by 1,000 Reformists with three cannon, 60 rifles with bayonets, and 260 small arms. Fortunately, a detachment of the Royal Canadian Rifle Regiment prevented further bloodshed by stopping either side from crossing Sappers Bridge, the only link between the two sections of the community. Needless to say, Lord Elgin chose not to come to Bytown that year. Four years later, however, in July 1853, he was given a hearty welcome.

It is hardly surprising that the decision in 1855 to change the name of Bytown to Ottawa was made at least in part to distance the evolving city from its checkered past and so to prepare it for its role as a singular seat of effective democracy. The new designation was fruitful. Only six years after the name change, Ottawa received its first laurel – it was said to be the healthiest place to live in all of British North America.

Green Island, like all of Ottawa, is the epitome of civility and serenity today. The striking shapes of City Hall and the great federal architecture to the south have transformed the place from industrial park to national treasure. Today, the mill of democracy grinds out law and order on the banks of the Rideau.

Much of Ottawa's prime real estate was close to the water's edge, but since the earliest days, was in the employ of the lumber barons. In 1925, Green Island (above) was still used as a lumber storage yard for the Edwards milling operations at Rideau Falls. This was soon to change all along the Ottawa. A quarter of a century later (below), the mills are gone and the yards bordering the river's edge have been developed for more national endeavours, such as the laboratories and offices of the National Research Council. Next to the NRC, one can clearly see Earnscliffe (originally the home of Sir John A. Macdonald) in the sparse tree canopy of early spring. Directly across a widened Sussex Drive, lies a residential area destined to be demolished, making way for the Macdonald-Cartier Bridge interchange.

As the 1960s came to a close, a new and high speed connection to Hull and Western Quebec (the Outaouais) had been completed. The Macdonald-Cartier Bridge, and the multi-lane highway it feeds, is a fast and direct route to the Gatineau Hills' ski resorts today. One can see that, by the end of that tumultuous decade, it had not yet made much of a penetration into these underdeveloped communities. The immense growth of residential development in the Outaouais over the past three decades is directly attributable to the ease of access afforded by this span.

These three aerial views reflect a forty year period from 1925 to the mid-60s. In the 1925 view we see the area, including Green Island in the Rideau River, devoted to the lumber industry. By the 1950s the National Research Council building has been completed at Sussex and King Edward, and it will serve as a visual anchor for many of the photos on these two pages. In the photo above we see finishing touches being applied to the new Macdonald-Cartier Bridge over the Ottawa River and the homes visible in the photo at left have all been expropriated and demolished to make way for the new Department of Foreign Affairs building visible in the colour photo at top left on the facing page..

Looking northwest to Hull, the Mcdonald-Cartier Bridge now connects two vibrant communities.

From heavy industrial site to magnificent parkland in seventy years. Though the original wild state of Green Island can never be reclaimed, the peaceful and ordered beauty of its parks and stately edifices is a municipal treasure.

24 Sussex Drive, the official residence of the Prime Minister of Canada, occupies the most spectacular site of all – a rocky promontory to the north of Green Island, where the river swings east.

As the Canada Day sun sets on a barely trickling Rideau Falls, three spectacular and patriotic hot air balloons compete for attention over Green Island and Ottawa City Hall.

As the balloons drift farther southward, they cross in front of the Lester B. Pearson Building, where Foreign Affairs diplomats host a Canada Day cocktail party on the terrace. From this exclusive vantagepoint, they have an exceptional view for the traditional fireworks, which dominate the sky over Entrance Bay each year.

During the summer months, the tumultuous cascade of spring diminishes to a mere trickle.

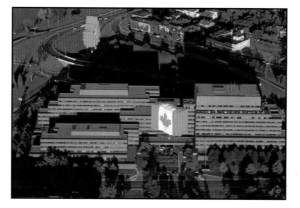

GREEN ISLAND
PRIVATE MOMENTS IN A PUBLIC PLACE

Green Island, site of Ottawa City Hall, the Minto Bridges and surrounding parklands, offers a tranquil respite in the heart of a bustling city. Like all of Ottawa's green spaces, Green Island is a place for all seasons. The long hot summer vibrant palette of nature is cause for wonder. When winter lays down her snow and ice, there are still hearty folks who don cross-country skis and take the dog for an outing. On the coldest day in February, it still warms the soul to

made all the more exhilarating after a bitter winter. Green Island, surrounded by fast moving water fed by melting snow, is one of the first places to come out of hibernation. Ottawans flock to the island and to Rideau Falls to

nights seem a lot cooler and more precious after a short stroll along Green Island's shores. When autumn comes, the contrast of City Hall's modern glass and steel (designed by legendary Canadian architect Moshe Safdie) with the stop and to watch the fading light, to see your breath on the cold air and to feel in your heart the quiet nature of your town. But truly, Ottawa's most magical season is springtime. It is a gift of life and warmth and fresh colour,

watch as winter's ice and snow runs at top speed over the escarpment and on out of their lives for yet another year. Soon, and seemingly over night, the trees are back again. A new green, a new Green Island, a fresh start.

ROCKCLIFFE PARK
QUIET ENCLAVE IN A BOOM TOWN

Soon after Thomas MacKay's arrival in Bytown, he began purchasing land. His biggest single tract was all the land that today underlies New Edinburgh, Rideau Hall and the Village of Rockcliffe Park. Once considered remote and inaccessible, the land beneath Rockcliffe Park is, for some, the most desirable in all the region. Here, the stately mansions, exotic gardens and manicured properties have created a mecca for the who's-who of Ottawa. A large number of Rockcliffe Park's exquisite homes are now occupied by consulates and the ambassadorial residences of many foreign countries. Despite the well-to-do occupants and the expensive homes in which they dwell, Rockcliffe Park carefully maintains a casual and somewhat rustic air. On most city streets, sidewalks are well maintained and an important part of the urban vernacular, but in Rockcliffe Park, you will not find any such public pedestrian thoroughfares. Perhaps this is to keep a certain country estate feel to the village. Perhaps it is to dissuade the hordes of strolling gawkers.

In addition to having many lush private gardens, Rockcliffe Park is surrounded by the most spectacular public parks in the region. In a natural glade along Hillsdale Road, daffodils, spring blossoms and lilacs turn a park into a painting.

Early morning sunlight glistens on dew-soaked spring blossoms in Rockcliffe Park.

NATIONAL AIR PHOTO LIBRARY IN.A.16.19

Only 75 years ago, Rockcliffe Park was much less developed than today. From the open cockpit of a biplane, we see only a few homes, where today there are scores. The Rockcliffe Boat House (upper left) still exists and the few homes seen in this picture can still be found amidst the raging fall colours on the facing page.

In the eight decades since the aerial photo at left was taken, the estates of Rockcliffe Park have divided and subdivided again and again - each new smaller piece selling for more than the whole from which it was partitioned. The village continues a highly controlled and slow development to this day, but still, throughout all the building, the aristocratic-yet-casual sensibility of the place has been maintained. For those who care about such things, there are no more prestigious addresses than those of Rockcliffe Park.

DOW'S LAKE
FROM SWAMP TO BUSINESS TO PLEASURE

Braddish Billings was the first and only settler along the Rideau River for almost six years. While conducting business upstream at Merrickville, he met Lamira Dow whom he was to marry and bring to Bytown. Not long thereafter a relative of Lamira, Abraham Dow, also came to Bytown from Merrickville (followed shortly thereafter by his two brothers, Samuel and Marbel) and settled along the same stretch of the Rideau. Part of the property on which he settled was a seemingly useless beaver pond and cedar swamp soon known as Dow's Great Swamp. When Colonel By was tasked with crossing this bog, he contracted Philemon Wright to construct a long dike that in turn flooded the swamp. The lake that was created became Dow's Lake and the embankment that By and his engineers laboured so hard to build is today the roadbed for the scenic parkway known as Colonel By Drive.

Dow's Lake is now the epicentre of recreational life along the Rideau Canal. On beautiful summer evenings and on sunny weekends, Dow's Lake is inundated with strollers, rowers, cyclists, joggers, in-line skaters, sailors and tour boats in a three-ring circus of urban delights. Along the northern shore, Commissioner's Park, the centrepeice of the tulips of the Canadian Tulip Festival, beckons picnickers, camera-toting tourists and lovers. To the left, the new pavilion known as Dow's Lake Marina attracts yachts from near and far. At the lower right, lies the unmistakable earthen dike, built by Colonel John By in 1830, which allowed the creation of the lake and over which automobiles and tour buses travel today.

Much has changed at Dow's Lake since the 1920's. From high above we clearly see that the north end of Dow's Lake is still a holding for milled lumber. This industrial site has since been transformed into a peaceful and mature residential enclave. The single-most striking aspect of this aerial is the arrow-straight causeway which cuts diagonally across the lake to circumvent the yards. When the water is drained from the canal system in the late fall, remnants of this roadway can still be seen. The rail line, which cuts across the canal northward to the Ottawa River, still carries freight, but the swing bridge and elevated railbed have long gone, replaced by a less obtrusive tunnel (built in 1967), which takes trains under the canal to emerge at Carling Avenue. As well, private boathouses once lined the embankment, which now forms the edge of the Arboretum.

The Central Experimental Farm, operated by Agriculture Canada, is an agricultural laboratory dedicated to crop and animal research. Not many large cities in the world can boast a fully functional farm right in their urban hearts.

Just down the river from Mooney's Bay lies the bustling and scenically located campus of Carleton University. In April, when students should be studying for final exams, the warm sunshine of the first sweet days of spring lures them outdoors.

NATIONAL AIR PHOTO LIBRARY IH.A.40.45

In this aerial taken in 1922, we can see that Hog's Back and Mooney's Bay were truly outside of town. Today, the fields, which once lined the river, have disappeared under residential neighbourhoods.

Mooney's Bay
Ottawa's summer playground

The changes that 75 years can generate in a community are clearly visible when comparing the old aerial view (above) with a contemporary line of sight. The city has grown southward from Carling Avenue and Dow's Lake, where it seems to have ended in 1923. The vast green spaces of Vincent Massey Park (centre), The Central Experimental Farm (upper left), Carleton University (upper middle) and Mooney's Bay (right) combine to preserve much of the natural beauty enjoyed by Ottawans throughout this century. Much of this green space is part of the National Capital Commission's "Greenbelt", a cordon of land encircling the city that is protected from development. At the lower right, we can just see the beginning of the sand of Mooney's Bay Beach, a perennial favourite of sun worshippers and swimmers seeking respite during the sweltering summer weekends.

HOG'S BACK
WILD WATER IN THE WILDERNESS

In 1957, Hog's Back was on the very outskirts of the city. Sparsely populated, it featured only a portion of the recreational or commercial uses that draw people today. The intersection of Hog's Back Drive and Highway 16 (now Prince of Wales Drive) is no more than a small country crossroads with the mandatory service station and wrecker's yard. A closer inspection reveals that Hog's Back is as it has always been, a tourist attraction. Cars fill the parking lot above the falls and a newly built stretch of Colonel By Drive reaches north along the canal from the locks and lift bridge.

At any time of year, the falls at Hog's Back are a thrilling sight, but during the month-long surge of water that accompanies melting snow, it is particularly awe inspiring.

For millennia, the waters of the Rideau River have cascaded wildly over Hog's Back. In 1892, the exposed rock and raging water were much the same, but were now under the control of a dam, The dam was built as part of the Rideau Canal system in order to create calm water above the escarpment for boat traffic.

A thirty foot escarpment of exposed rock strata, pushed up by the forces of nature eons ago, is what we call Hog's Back today. In summer it is little more than a series of pools emptying from one to another.

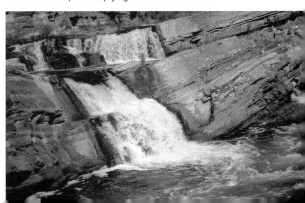

In a picture taken only forty years later than the one at left, we see tremendous change has come upon Hog's Back. No longer at the edge of town, it is now surrounded on all sides by the city. Much of what was originally there has been preserved however. Immediately across the Hog's Back gorge lies one of our premier parks - Vincent Massey Park (named for Canada's first native-born Governor General). Here, on any weekend afternoon, you will find hundreds of Ottawa families enjoying a picnic, a game of softball or an ice cream cone and a stroll along the falls. Recreation is the number one land use along the river. Above the falls lie the Mooney's Bay Marina, the Terry Fox track and field centre and Mooney's Bay Beach on the east side and the Rideau Canoe Club on the west side. The RCC is the site of the National Capital Dragon Boat Race Festival, held in June each year.

When summer comes, the water at the falls becomes gentler. For years, the falls in summer were a favourite high-diving spot for thrill-seeking youth. While such activity is strictly prohibited these days, it is still a relaxing spot for anglers to cast a line.

Looking west over Hog's Back to the large residential community, which has sprung up around Meadowlands Drive. Below, amidst the trees, we see the circular, pleated roof of Hog's Back Pavilion where, for years, families have come on hot summer days to enjoy an ice cream.

Looking north from the Heron Road Bridge along the Rideau Canal toward Carleton University, we see the different nature of the east and west bank of the waterway. The east is a solid wall of concrete, designed to hold back the earth that underpins the roadbed of Colonel By Drive. The west, along the edge of property owned by the Central Experimental Farm is, on the other hand, completely natural, much like the embankment along a creek.

Carleton University occupies a triangle of land between the Rideau River and the Rideau Canal. Carleton moved here in 1960 and has grown steadily around the main quadrangle garden in front of the high Arts Tower. Carleton offers degree programs in architecture, sciences, arts, commerce, engineering and is known across Canada for its excellent school of journalism. Adjacent to the site, the Rideau Canal makes the first step upwards since the headlocks at the Chateau Laurier. These are Hartwell's Locks, a two-stage, twenty-foot climb, which was constructed by Thomas MacKay. The stone lockmaster's house (west of the upper lock chamber), though now clad in wood clapboard, still stands where MacKay built it in the 19th century.

At Hartwell's Locks each spring, a dumpster load of yellow rubber ducks is dumped into the recently filled canal. Each bathtub duck has a number on its bottom corresponding with a number on a ticket purchased by a citizen of Ottawa. Thousands watch as the first duck crosses the finish line, making a winner out of the ticket holder. The prizes are fabulous and the proceeds benefit the Children's Hospital of Eastern Ontario.

On the east side of Carleton University, the Rideau River runs through a particularly fast stretch along the western perimeter of Vincent Massey Park. From early spring through to late fall, the river's edge is an attractive spot for those looking for respite from the chaos of city life. Here, in spring, you will find university students with anything but study on their minds.

This 1960 aerial offers a glimpse of the second birth of one of Ottawa's two major universities. Carleton University, which moved to the site from its original location in the Glebe is, at the time, comprised of only three buildings surrounding a landscaped quadrangle - the Maxwell MacOdrum Library (left), Patterson Hall arts building (middle) and Tory sciences building.

A water colour painted in 1835, shortly after Colonel By and his contractor Thomas Mackay completed Hartwell's Locks, shows little development on the land which is now occupied by Carleton University. In this view looking south toward Hog's Back, we can make out the inlet that still runs westward from the locks. A road, which we can see running along the west bank and the small bridge it crosses, have long since disappeared.

An apparition in the wilderness, like Fitzcarraldo on the Amazon. Such was the scene in 1844 and during much of the 19th century. Large flat-bottomed canal steamers churned their way along the waterway, accompanied by birch bark canoes. Much of Colonel By's canal was lined with trees right down to the waterline. How sweet it would be if we could travel back in time to sit upon the bank under the shade of the dark, virgin forest. We would watch as one of these great side-wheel steamers slowly rounds a downstream bend, southbound for Westport, and listen to the thrashing wheel, the puffing steam engine and hear the shouts of the pilot.

NEVER THOUGHT OF FLOWER POWER

THE SPECIAL RELATIONSHIP THAT EXISTS BETWEEN THE
PEOPLE OF OTTAWA AND THE DUTCH ROYAL FAMILY HAS —
QUITE LITERALLY — BLOSSOMED, SINCE THE SECOND
WORLD WAR.

When Holland was invaded by the Nazis in 1940, Crown Princess
Juliana found shelter for herself and her two daughters, Beatrix and
Irene, in Ottawa. They first lived in a stone house on the banks of
MacKay Lake in Rockcliffe Park, where the grieving princess named
their temporary residence *Noot Gedach* (Never Thought). They soon
settled down, however, and the princess lived a simple life, working for
various war efforts, shunning private education for the young royals in
favour of sending them to the local elementary school and, on occasion,
shoveling her own snow. Prince Bernhard, who commanded the Dutch
Military Mission in England, managed to visit his family several times.

Princess Margriet, the National Capital's very own royal princess, was
born on January 19th, 1943 at the Ottawa Civic Hospital. The delivery
room was declared Netherlands' territory for that day and, for the first
time in history, a foreign flag — the Royal Standard of the House of
Orange — was flown from the Peace Tower on Parliament Hill. On
returning to Holland at war's end, a grateful Juliana sent 20,000 tulip
bulbs to the city, "for services rendered in time of need," and every year
since then many more thousands of bulbs have followed, giving rise to
the largest tulip festival in the world, the Canadian Tulip Festival.

Each May since 1951, this spectacular festival has provided an eye-
popping opportunity for the people of Ottawa and countless visitors to
celebrate both the much-anticipated arrival of spring and the
importance of international friendship — expressed, in this case, in the
universal language of flowers.

*A single tulip blazes in the warm sunlight of early May. Soon, its numbers will swell into the millions,
until it seems the entire length of the canal is blanketed in fabulous colour. Ottawans, Canadians and
tourists from as far away as Japan come to enjoy Princess Juliana's gift, to take a picture amidst the
blooms and to stroll through the endless sea of colour. Though a tradition born of tragedy over fifty
years ago, the tulip has become, like the Peace Tower and the Guardsman, an icon of Canada's Capital.*

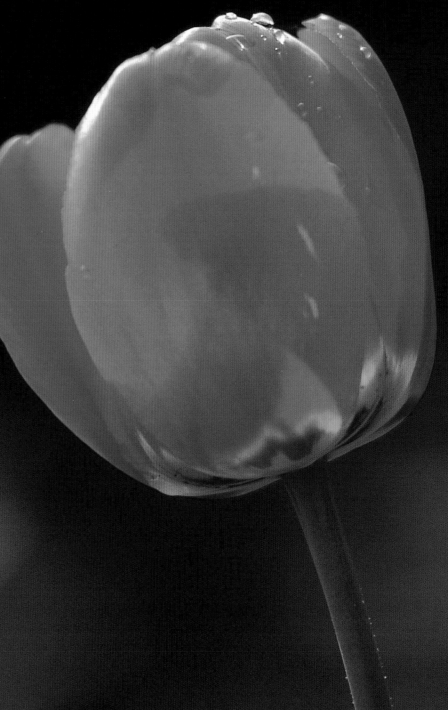

All along the canal, the tulip reigns supreme, when the warm May sun forces their heads up after another long winter. The show is brief, with only a couple of weeks of prime colour before the bulbs are removed and the summer annuals planted in their stead. For those short weeks, the citizens of Ottawa vie with tourists from around the world for the best unobstructed camera angles on the fiery display. The Canadian Tulip Festival is scheduled to coincide with the blooming of the tulips, but after a particularly mild winter, the tulips can be out and gone before the ribbon is cut. Such are the risks of holding an outdoor festival, but that does not deter organizers. When the gates open and the music kicks in, Ottawans come out to work out the stiffness of the long winter months.

During the Nazi occupation of Holland in WWII, part of the Dutch Royal Family lived in Ottawa. The distant war in their homeland surely weighed heavily on the Royals, but the gracious and warmhearted hospitality of Ottawans kept their spirits up until repatriation. Relaxing outside their temporary Ottawa home in the summer of 1942 are Queen Wilhemina (left), her daughter Princess Juliana and her two grand-daughters Princesses Beatrix and Irene. Queen Wilhemina was just visiting, for she, along with Juliana's husband Prince Bernhard, spent the war years at the Dutch Mission in London, England.

One of the high points for Ottawans during the war years was the birth of Dutch Princess Margriet to Princess Juliana. After her christening Crown Princess Juliana and Prince Bernhard of the Netherlands show off Princess Margriet to the throngs of photographers outside Saint Andrews Church in Ottawa.

The tulip has become for Ottawans, a symbol of friendship, hope and strength and when spring comes, a symbol of rebirth.

In 1951, the annual gift of tulips inspired several Ottawa businessmen, including renowned tulip photographer Malak Karsh, to inaugurate a yearly Tulip Festival.
On the fortieth anniversary of the Canadian Tulip Festival, Crown Princess Margriet and her husband returned to the place of her birth as the special guest of the festival she inspired. There, during the Spring Flotilla, she travelled down the Rideau Canal aboard a tour boat, while many thousands of Ottawans lined the canal to greet her.

The tulip is not a native Dutch flower. In fact, over four hundred years ago, a Dutch businessman and exporter brought back to Holland, from Turkey, a ship full of examples of this spectacular flower for cultivation.
To Turks, the tulip is a national symbol like the maple leaf is to Canadians. It adorns their mosaics, their tapestries and carpets and even, as does our own maple leaf, the tails of the aircraft of their national airline. The gift of hospitality and freedom, which Ottawans gave the Dutch, has through them, translated into a growing friendship with the wonderful people of Turkey. Where else will it take us?

OTTAWA'S AIRPORT PREVAILING WINDS OF CHANGE

In 1927, Canada was in its sixtieth year. The highlight of a two-day Diamond Jubilee celebration in Ottawa was a special goodwill visit by Charles Lindbergh. At the time, "Lucky Lindy" was a hero of unprecedented proportions. Only six weeks before, he had completed his historic non-stop solo flight across the Atlantic. His arrival in Ottawa, so shortly after, was an honour for all Canadians and thousands turned out to greet him. Lindbergh, flying his legendary Ryan monoplane, the 'Spirit of St. Louis', was escorted by a flight of twelve fighter aircraft from the 27th Squadron the First Pursuit Group of the US Army Air Corps. The large formation met up with three additional aircraft of the newly formed Royal Canadian Air Force, which were based at Rockcliffe, and the group flew around the Peace Tower and then south to a makeshift airfield prepared near The Ottawa Hunt Club.

Lindbergh landed there to be greeted by cheering crowds, but the joy soon turned to horror when two of the USAAC fighters collided in mid-air. The pilot of one of the aircraft, Captain Thad Johnson of Michigan, bailed out, but was too low for his

parachute to open before he struck the ground. Though he was visibly upset by the death of Johnson, Lindbergh continued on in to Ottawa to help celebrate the Jubilee. The next day, Prime Minister King cancelled celebrations and ordered a state funeral for the fallen American. He was then taken by a special funeral train to his home in Michigan. As the train left Ottawa along the Canal, Lindbergh made repeated passes over the track to drop flowers in his honour. Today, an internal road on the airport grounds bears the name of the unfortunate American aviator.

The 'Spirit of St. Louis' is perhaps the most famous aircraft in history. When Lindbergh landed in Ottawa in 1927, it was leading-edge technology, and thousands wanted a glimpse. Two young women (left) pose with the Ryan monoplane, while Canadian Army and Air Force officers take a closer look at the cockpit. Today, this very aircraft hangs from the ceiling of the Smithsonian National Air and Space Museum in Washington.

High above the rough airfield on the Uplands, we see thousands have gathered to catch a glimpse of the most famous man in the world. A picture is worth a thousand words and close inspection reveals the 'Spirit of St. Louis' parked at the southeast end (right) of the shorter runway. Along the edge of that runway towards the spot where it intersects with the longer one, we see lined up, eleven of the twelve American fighter aircraft which escorted 'The Lone Eagle' to Ottawa. The twelfth, piloted by Captain Thad Johnson crashed while attempting a landing. Even closer inspection reveals thousands waiting along the Bowesville Road for Lindbergh's entourage to drive into town. At the very bottom of this picture, we also find a large group of people gathered around an object outside the perimeter fence - perhaps Captain Johnson's aircraft.

The field near the Hunt Club became known for a while as Lindbergh Field and people inspired by Lindy's visit formed the Ottawa Flying Club in 1928. As aviation grew, so did Ottawa's airport. Here, more than seventy years earlier is the site of Lindbergh's tragedy-marred arrival. During WWII, this field and its runways were part of the British Commonwealth Air Training Program. Today it is known as the "North Field" of the Ottawa International Airport and is still the home of the Ottawa Flying Club. Though this part of the airport does not handle any airline traffic, it remains very busy to this day with general aviation services such as training, hangaring, maintenance and sightseeing.

The Ottawa International Airport today is a city unto itself. Fast food restaurants, bars, banking, bookstores and other businesses combine to take advantage of a captive clientele with anywhere from five minutes to five hours to spare. Ottawa, not being one of the big airline hubs, enjoys quick turnarounds and minimal delays for its passengers.

In 1945, after nearly five years in exile, the Royal Family of the Netherlands is together again in Ottawa. Prince Bernhard (right) and his mother Queen Wilhemina have arrived to join the family, prior to returning to Holland. His three daughters (Irene left, Beatrix center and little Margriet) walk across the infield of RCAF Station Uplands, while Princess Juliana welcomes the Queen.

In 1954, Canadians still looked upon airline travel as the sole privilege of the rich and famous. The passengers' waiting lounge at the Ottawa Airport in 1954 clearly shows us that few passengers were passing through its doors. A few chairs, a soft drink machine and a schedule rack make this lounge look more like a bus terminal in a deserted prairie town. Within a few years, things would change drastically.

By 1960, Ottawa Airport had a brand new International-style terminal building. In the days before sky-jackings and terrorist bombs, relatives who came to see-off passengers or greet them when they returned, could do so from either the "Sunken Gardens" or the rooftop terrace. The "Sunken Gardens" (V-shaped terrace between the two departure wings) was an outdoor viewing area about three feet below the level of the airport ramp. From here well-wishers could talk to departing passengers who were expected to walk outdoors to their airliner in all weather conditions. When the departing aircraft swung around to taxi to the active runway, its prop-wash would blow grit and hot fumes right in the faces of folks waving goodbye. Here we see two British-built Vickers Viscount aircraft of the type flown by Trans Canada Airlines (soon to become Air Canada).

The modern control tower for YOW (three-letter international code for Ottawa's airport) replaced the old one in the 1980s. It stands alone in the infield at the intersection of the two main runways. The old tower (above) can still be seen buried in the modern complex (facing page left of the central atrium) and is now used for gate control and assignment.

Lindbergh and Johnson would be amazed at what has taken place on that scrubby pasture they flew over in 1927. The large, modern airport still retains the shape of its 1960s predecessor but has expanded in every direction. In the background on "Delta" taxiway stand the hangar facilities for the RCMP aviation services (far right) and the National Research Council's flight research laboratory (right of centre). At left and above lies the land once occupied by the enormous air force base called Uplands. In the 1990s the need for the base disappeared and since then almost all of the hangars and buildings of this historic airfield have been demolished. At upper left stands one of the remaining hangars, Number 11, which now houses the Canada Reception Centre, where heads-of-state disembark their aircraft, with much fanfare, for the limousine ride into town. In fact, if Lindbergh were to arrive today, this is the place to which he would taxi the 'Spirit of St.Louis'.

BILLINGS' BRIDGE

PREVAILING WINDS OF CHANGE

In 1924, road construction involved horsepower of two kinds. A ditch digging steam shovel drops a bucket of earth into a horse-drawn wagon along Bowesville Road (now called Riverside Drive) near the present day site of Billings' Bridge.

Tired horses could be led to water along the Rideau River, and it didn't take much prodding to get them to drink either. Looking north along the river from the site of present day Rideau River Park, the original bridge was visible in the background in 1910.

In 1957, the Billings' Bridge area was beginning to become a major commercial crossroads, but back in the first decade of the 19th century, it was raw wilderness. When Braddish Billings, the son of a United Empire Loyalist who once worked for Philemon Wright, first set eyes on it in 1809, he knew he would go into the lumber business himself. Within two years he had cleared several acres and built himself a log cabin. To this day, part of the stone wall of his fireplace can still be seen in a park along Riverside Drive beside the bridge. Billings was the first settler in all of Gloucester Township and his economic grip over the area lasted for many years. His large estate on the hill to the southeast is now owned and maintained by the City of Ottawa.

To this day, Billings' Bridge (especially the embankments at Windsor and Brantwood Park) is a good place to slip your canoe into the stream for a leisurely paddle after dinner. In 1916 a "Miss Loper" demonstrates perfect paddling technique and the latest in recreational fashion. In the background lies Billings' Bridge, which was operated as a toll bridge back then. The white wood structure at the end of the bridge is the tollhouse.

Old Braddish Billings could not have imagined what a commercial artery Bank street would become as it crossed his bridge and climbed the long hill south. Today, Billings' Bridge Shopping Centre, one of Ottawa's first in the early 1960s, stands on the open land cleared by Braddish Billings himself. But it wasn't the first major enterprise to occupy his land. Before the property was given over to parking lots and retail, there once stood, on the very same spot, a large factory of the Ottawa Brick Company. Many homes in the Glebe and other Ottawa neighbourhoods are constructed from a distinctive soft red clay brick of the type manufactured at this factory. The large and shabby brick kilns and abandoned buildings were torn down to make room for modern progress in the form of shopping.

High up behind Billings' Bridge Shopping Centre, lies a rail line and a major public transportation station. Here, buses from many south Ottawa routes hook up with uptown buses in one of the busiest nodes in the Region's rapid transit system. The rail line, which crosses Bank Street, has existed for many years and is now used exclusively for VIA passenger travel from Ottawa to Toronto and beyond. Rail has a special place in the history of Billings Bridge, for it was only as far as here that the first rail line to the city came. Funding for the line from Prescott simply dried up and Billings Bridge was as far as the line could go. Excited citizens of New Edinburgh, who desperately wanted the first train to come farther up the river to their village, were forced to use ingenious methods. MacKay and his people completed the line themselves using 3" x 3" dressed hardwood rails laid across two miles of frozen fields. In the winter of 1854, a chuffing locomotive named "Oxford" crept over the creaking and shifting track and steamed slowly into New Edinburgh to much fanfare.

NATIONAL ARCHIVES OF CANADA / PA-122219

View from atop the rail bridge in 1923 looking north along Bank Street towards the river. The street is modern and widened to accept growing automobile traffic, but the setting is decidedly bucolic.

The same view today, but further up the hill and looking under the bridge. Only a few years ago, the old rail trestle was replaced with a new combination rapid transit and rail bridge which blocks much of the view. While Billings' Bridge can no longer be considered pretty in any way, its importance as a transportation and commercial hub remains undiminished.

HULL
REACHING ACROSS THE RIVER

BRIDGES – VIRTUAL AND REAL

A STRONG BOND HAS ALWAYS CONNECTED THE NATIONAL CAPITAL WITH ITS COMPANION CITY ACROSS THE OTTAWA RIVER – HULL.

John Burrows Honey arrived from England in 1817 to take possession of 80 hectares (200 acres) of desolate swamp and cedar bush immediately south of what is now Ottawa's Parliament Hill. He built his cabin where Wellington and Lyon streets intersect today and he sought work in the nearest community – Philemon Wright's town on the other side of the river. Thus, commuting between Ottawa and Hull began with Mr. Honey almost two centuries ago and has expanded from one person per day (and no bridge) in 1817 to more than 150,000 people a day (and five bridges) at the start of the 21st century.

The sculpted landscaping of Nepean Point stands above the treed pedestrian concourse at Alexandra Bridge.

For decades after the Great fire of 1900, Hull suffered from its effects. Homes that were destroyed by the fire were those of the working class families employed by the mills. Compensation was barely enough to close in a new home and for seventy years many of the houses in the downtown area remained virtually unfinished. Tar paper and rough stucco became part of the vernacular of old Hull, which resembled a shantytown more than a major urban centre. Today, a revitalized downtown core with excellent restaurants, public parks and restored buildings makes the city of Hull a vibrant part of the Nation's Capital region.

A major part in the rebirth of the City of Hull was the decision to locate the Canadian Museum of Civilization to the old Eddy pulp mill site along the Ottawa River at Entrance Bay. This had the effect of anchoring positive development and bridging the river with the Nation's Capital. Not long after came the announcement that the government of Québec would build a world class casino at the old quarry near Leamy Lake. This spectacular and tasteful structure attracts tourists and citizens alike. In summer, the flooded quarry comes alive with towering fountains and a festival of fireworks that rivals Canada Day.

Nine years after the commuting tradition was introduced, the first stone of the very first bridge to link the two sides of the river was laid. In fact, in impressive testimony to the absence of bureaucratic red tape, the bridge was begun the same day that construction was ordered – September 27th, 1826. Its original purpose was to accommodate the flow of men and materials between Wright's community on the north shore and the Rideau Canal construction site on the south. The 192 metre (640 foot) long, nine metre (30 foot) wide, eight-span Union Bridge – it was the first bridge to unite Upper and Lower Canada – hopped island-to-island across the seething Chaudière, its spans arched sufficiently to escape anticipated seven metre (24 foot) high spring floods.

The following year in embryonic Ottawa, a stone bridge reached across the deep cut of the Rideau Canal, linking the western end of Lower Town's Rideau Street to a wagon trail that first wound its way for almost three-quarters of a kilometre around the south side of Barracks (Parliament) Hill before joining Wellington Street in Upper Town. Eighty-five years later, dynamite couldn't budge this structure. When Sappers' Bridge was being demolished to make way for the Grand Trunk Railway's Union Station (now slated to become home to the Canadian Sports Hall of Fame) and the Chateau Laurier Hotel (whose 1912 grand opening was delayed by the drowning of railway president Charles Hays in the Titanic disaster), a two-ton boulder had to be dropped from a height of 15 metres (50 feet) for more than three hours before the bridge collapsed.

Today, Ottawa and the whole National Capital Region is a living bridge, one that unites Canada's francophone, anglophone, indigenous and immigrant communities. It was settled by the people of the nation's two founding cultures on the site of an ancient aboriginal meeting place and then matured to near-perfection by the drive and passion of those who followed from around the globe. Ottawa, heart of the village, essence of Canada.

CITY OF OTTAWA ARCHIVES / CA-0278

CITY OF OTTAWA ARCHIVES

In the early 1950s and right up to the 1970s, the land across the river from Parliament Hill was dedicated to the forest industry. Throughout the spring and summer months, logs floated down river to be collected in booms at Entrance Bay. These were towed to the enormous log conveyors, where lumberjacks fed their contents either into the mill or to mountainous log piles behind. The piles would get particularly huge with winter approaching, as the mill struggled to get enough pulpwood to keep them busy when the river was frozen. Day or night throughout the fall, you could see the endless stream of logs falling from the conveyors to crash and tumble down the face of the mountain. Forever present was the sound of screeching and booming and the smell of the sulphur used in the making of pulp.

The sheds and factories of the great Hull mills swept along the shore from Alexandra Bridge all the way to the Chaudière Falls. Victoria Island midstream was occupied by both mills and the facilities of National Defence Construction Ltd..

From an aerial vantagepoint to the southwest of Chaudière Falls, we see the sweep of the river and four of the five bridges that join the two halves of the National Capital region. From the newest to the oldest, they represent a physical statement of the unity sought by all Canadians. At the top and ascending up-river, we have the Macdonald-Cartier, Alexandra or Interprovincial, the Portage and the Chaudière Bridges. The complex dams and sluices of the still functioning E.B. Eddy mills mask the Chaudière Bridge and its series of spans.

The Canadian Museum of Civilization, designed by renowned Canadian architect Douglas Cardinal, is the jewel in the crown of Hull's redevelopment. The evocative curvelinear forms and use of natural materials bring to mind the essence of the land, of history and of Canada. Cardinal's unique Métis perspective has created a design in harmony with the spirit of the place, for it was right here, only two centuries ago, that his forefathers, both native and French, made camp.

The beautiful lines of the Canadian Museum of Civilization look more a part of the land than of the skyline. Since the creation of this world-class museum, the entire edge of the river has been revitalized. A landscaped path now enables people to completely circumnavigate Entrance Bay on foot or bicycle.

The busy pulp mill at the site of today's Canadian Museum of Civilization dominated life and sight across from Parliament Hill for many years. In the 1950s, it was producing at its peak. The great mountains of pulpwood logs, put up for the winter, were gone by springtime, when the harvest started all over again. Acquiring the property, owned by the E.B. Eddy company, was a long-time goal of Douglas Fullerton, then the Chairman of the National Capital Commission. There is an urban legend around his negotiations for the sale of the mill and forty acres along the water. In 1972, he was in Paris where he met company officials. The legend tells how he wrote a personal cheque for the land right on the spot without confirming with NCC officials, then caught the next plane home to arrange for the money.

Beyond the log piles we see the grey stone walls of the Grey Nuns Normal School, which still exists today (see inset). The Grey Nuns from Montreal were first sent to Bytown in 1854 to help with the spiritual and physical welfare of the growing town. Their first Sister Superior, Elizabeth Bruyère, started the nucleus of what would soon become the Ottawa General Hospital. The General moved from its site in the 1980s and the building became the Elizabeth Bruyère Center, a chronic care facility for the aging.

A MATCHLESS EVOLUTION

REVERSE GENDER DISCRIMINATION PROTECTED WOMEN WHO, IN 1875, HAND-DIPPED ONE MILLION MATCH HEADS A DAY AT THE E.B. EDDY MATCH FACTORY ON THE BANKS OF THE OTTAWA RIVER.

Because of the high risk of combustion, it was a man who was given the honour of being employed to blend the match head coating mixture. He did this by pouring the volatile ingredients into a bucket, stepping onto a springboard, and jumping up and down with the bucket grasped firmly between his (shaking?) knees.

Towards the end of the 19th century, E.B. Eddy branched out into paper making, foreseeing the dependence of an expanding government bureaucracy on its plentiful supply. Today, the Eddy company still plays an important role in the community, but it is the makers of virtual paper – world leaders in computer technology – who have reincarnated Ottawa. No longer a sleepy government town, the National Capital is now a hotbed of originality in the advanced sciences.

There are few festivals around the world more visually spectacular than the Gatineau Hot Air Balloon Festival, which takes place in late summer over the city of Gatineau. Gatineau is a paper mill town and bedroom community to the east of Hull. Each year the city is host to "Le Festival de montgolfières de Gatineau". "Montgolfières", the proper French word for hot air balloons, is a word with tremendous historic importance for the French. In the 18th century, two French brothers, Joseph and Etienne Montgolfier (coincidentally paper makers), made the first manned ascent in a hot air balloon.

The festival is now into its second decade and it has grown to be one of the world's largest. The centrepieces of the event are the twice-daily mass balloon launches – one at sunrise and one before sundown. Over 100 hot air balloons of all shapes, sizes and colours (giant cows, eagles, Mounties, light bulbs, champagne bottles etc) take to the air and spread out across the horizon. Over 200,000 citizens from both sides of the river take part in the four days of festivities at Gatineau's Parc de la baie, but hundreds of thousands more across the city watch from whatever vantagepoint they can. Conditions look good for a launch – setting sun, unlimited visibility and light winds from the northwest about to carry the balloons over the

Throughout the entire region, the tumbling waters of our rivers and streams have provided the nucleus for development of our communities big and small – from E.B. Eddy's huge factories at Chaudière Falls to the small stone mill at Wakefield, Québec. Wakefield, a former mill and quarry town up the Gatineau River from Hull, is now one of the most popular tourist destinations in the region. Excellent restaurants, skiing, boutiques and bakeries make the scenic thirty-minute drive even more worthwhile.

The former O'Brian Residence on Meech Lake was the site of the failed Meech Lake Accord. In the 1970s it was refurbished as an elite parliamentary conference centre.

The Wakefield Steam Train runs all summer long along the old rail bed on the west bank of the Gatineau River. Steam enthusiasts, tourists and local families take the twice-daily slow, rolling trip from Hull through Chelsea to Wakefield.

Golfers putt out at the 7th hole of the Larrimac Golf and Country Club. One of the Ottawa region's oldest courses, Larrimac, celebrating its 75th anniversary in 1999, offers nine of the most scenic holes in the Gatineaus.

While the engine is turned around at the hand-operated turntable, passengers disembark for some sightseeing and shopping in the picturesque lakeside town of Wakefield.

KINGSMERE

ECCENTRIC BEAUTY IN A SUBLIME SETTING

In 1950, the more than 600-acre estate of the late Prime Minister William Lyon MacKenzie King was turned over to the federal government. The property, known as Kingsmere, was immediately incorporated into plans for development of the Gatineau Park region. At the heart of King's land was his summer residence, Moorside, which today functions as a teahouse and interpretive centre for the estate. Since King was unmarried and without heirs, he left this wonderful, silent woodland and its recuperative qualities for all Canadians to enjoy as he did during the most turbulent years of his leadership. He would be very happy to see that his wish has been carried out and that Canadians have come to consider it their own.

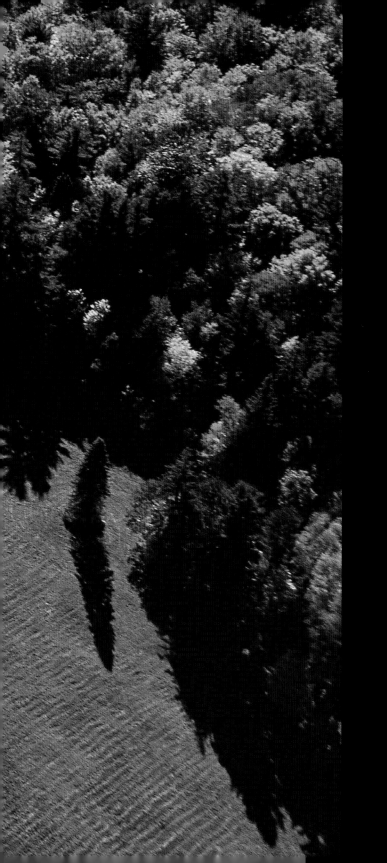

Winter or summer, Kingsmere and Moorside have qualities that make them uniquely Canadian – natural, pristine, silent and elegant. In winter, cross-country skiers and snowshoers take advantage of the snowy setting to cast off the accumulated stresses of big city living.

The ruins of Kingsmere, born from the creative mind of a great man, now stand year round as a tribute to his beliefs, his love of family and his personal history. In summer, thousands stop to see and understand. In winter, only intrepid naturalists and the animals of the forest come to share a moment with his spirit. King would probably like the winter visitors best of all.

Nobody would deny that William Lyon MacKenzie King was an eccentric sort. Given to communing with his dead mother and the spirit of Wilfred Laurier and chats with his dog, the confirmed bachelor loved to retire to the peace and serenity of Kingsmere. A closet spiritualist, King enjoyed meditation in the confines of his private ruins. Erected as a ruin, the structure was concocted with components from various meaningful sources – the old printing shop of his grandfather, the original Parliament Buildings which were destroyed by fire in 1916 and even the Parliament Buildings in London, England.

How To Spot A Capital-ist And Other Sporting Tales

CITY OF OTTAWA ARCHIVES / CA-4110

It's the bottom of the first. Already the Ottawa Athletics are down three runs to visiting Buffalo, but now the home team swats one over the fence at Lansdowne Park and on to Queen Elizabeth Drive. In 1898, long before the coming of the Ottawa Lynx, the city was home to a Triple A baseball team of the International League, but the city was not ready for the sport and the team folded in a year. They were back again in 1951 as the Ottawa Giants, the farm team of the New York Giants. The next year, they became part of the Philadelphia Athletics organization and their name was changed appropriately. The diamond was laid down across the football field and homeplate was on the north side. This photo was taken sometime after 1952, but the team was disbanded in the same decade and Ottawa had to wait forty years before the return of high calibre baseball.

The 1996 Ottawa Lynx, farm team of the Montreal Expos the 1995 International League Champions.

NATIVES OF THE NATIONAL CAPITAL WERE BETRAYED BY THEIR GAIT, ACCORDING TO AN EARLY 20TH CENTURY CHRONICLER OF THE CITY. "SKATING... GIVES GRACE AND FIRMNESS OF STEP, ACQUIRED IN NO OTHER WAY," WROTE HISTORIAN ANSON GARD IN 1904. "AND SINCE ALL OTTAWANS SKATE — AS IN NO OTHER CITY IN THE WORLD IS IT SO GENERAL — IT FOLLOWS THAT THE OTTAWA STEP IS UNIQUE."

He made this observation as a crowd of spectators strode smartly uptown after the home team had won the 1903 national hockey championship trophy, the coveted Stanley Cup. The city went on to capture the title a total of eight more times within three decades — three times as the Silver Seven and six as the Ottawa Senators — before the team disbanded in 1934. However, Canada's national sport returned triumphantly to the National Capital in 1992, with the rebirth of the Senators and their re-entry into the National Hockey League.

Not all Senators games were played on ice in the 1920s. For three years of that decade there were two local teams sporting the patrician name, one of which propelled a pigskin, not a puck.

In 1925, the city's 50-year-old football team won its first national championship, the Grey Cup, just one year after changing its name from the Ottawa Rough Riders to the Senators. This long-awaited success was remarkably repeated the following year, but the team appears to have thumbed its nose at Lady Luck in 1927 by reverting once more to its original name and was to capture only seven more championships in as many decades before sadly dissolving in 1996.

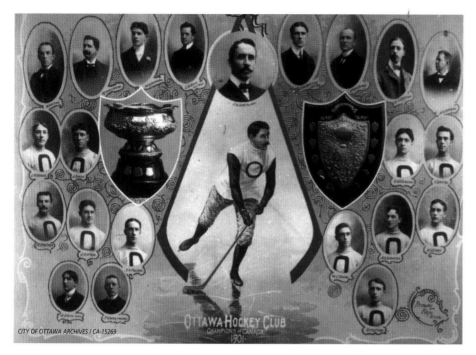

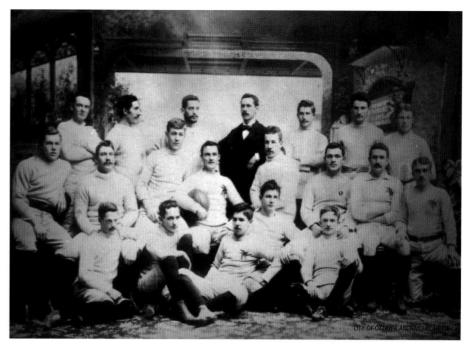

The 1901 Ottawa Silver Seven, Canadian and Stanley Cup Champions for the second time in two years.

The 1892 Ottawa Football Club became know as the "Rough Riders" in 1898.

The 1999 Ottawa 67's Junior A team of the Ontario Hockey League, thrilling 1999 Memorial Cup winners.

The 1999 Ottawa Senators, Northeast Divisional Champions of the National Hockey League.

In the 19th Century, the opening of a new indoor skating rink was as big an event as the opening of the Corel Centre. In a town with not too much going on throughout the winter, the event took on even more importance. In attendance at the opening of the rink on Laurier Avenue, were Ottawa's elite – lumber barons, Members of Parliament and businessmen and their families. The stuffy old barons and MPs stand to the left, as women, children and rakish young men swirl on the ice surface, accompanied by waltzes from a band on the balcony above. Overhead in the rafters, the bunting and banners hang in the mist generated by the huge crowd. Even a photographer of William James Topley's skill, could not get everyone to stand still for long enough, so he resorted to a little 19th century cut and paste to create the scene.

Ottawa today has literally dozens of modern indoor skating rinks, most of which maintain ice year round. In addition, there are many more municipally operated outdoor rinks, which grace every neighbourhood in winter. The flagship arena of the region is the 18,500-seat Corel Centre, home to the NHL's Ottawa Senators. As in the last century, the who's-who of Ottawa turned out for its spectacular opening. Instead of stiff lumber barons, the celebration was attended by the new, more colourful captains of industry – such as Michael Cowpland and Rod Bryden, the helmsmen of Ottawa's high technology juggernaut. Canadian rock legend Bryan Adams provided the music. Originally called the Palladium, it would, within the year, be known by its present name. Two streets, which were built to access this $170 million facility, were named for two of the brightest stars of the Stanley Cup winning Ottawa Senators of old – Cyclone Taylor Boulevard and Frank Finnegan Way.

When the winter months settle over Ottawa's streets, the timid head south to warmer climes and the brave-hearted embrace the best things that it has to offer. From the observation deck of the Peace Tower, a lone photographer captures the silent freeze that engulfs Entrance Bay. The green stained copper roof of the Parliamentary Library frames the ice on former Sleigh Bay far below, where the sleighs of the Philemon Wright wedding party stood 175 years ago. The two inset photos, both taken from the ill-fated Victoria Tower, show us how this area has changed over the years.

Before 1900 (far left), one had to cross at Chaudière in order to get to the other half of the region. Nepean Point is still largely underdeveloped, and the activity at Fitzgibbon's Landing, at the foot of the locks, seems to have resulted in severe pollution.

Around 1910 (left), the brand new Alexandra Bridge, named for then Queen Alexandra, spans the gap. The surface of Nepean Point is a well-groomed park, with overlooks and pavilions, reached by a footbridge from Major's Hill Park. In the background, the new Royal Canadian Mint and Public Archives are in full operation.

Today, the Market in winter is a place many Ottawans from downtown neighbourhoods go to get their Christmas trees and firewood. But on Christmas Day, 1998, everyone is at home with the fire lit and the presents under the tree. This view is identical to that in the historic photograph at centre below.

WINTER
LOVE IT OR LEAVE IT

Firewood, Christmas trees and Christmas dinner have been part of winter in the Byward Market for over a century. Despite the obvious cold, or maybe because of it, woodsellers (left) do a brisk business at the corner of William and Clarence in 1918. Somehow, the idea of picking up the family Christmas tree by horse drawn sleigh seems much more poetic than tossing it in the trunk of the family car, as seen in this image taken on December 23, 1926. In the days before frozen pre-basted turkeys, the Market offered the freshest possible Christmas turkeys and geese. Fowlers sold their wares, freshly plucked, with the heads still attached.

John Boyd / NATIONAL ARCHIVES OF CANADA / PA-087686

NATIONAL ARCHIVES OF CANADA / PA-070983

John Boyd / NATIONAL ARCHIVES OF CANADA / PA-087687

CANADIAN SKI MUSEUM

(Below) Rather than making their way to the Gatineaus for some downhill thrills, skiers took to the short but steep slopes near Rockcliffe Park in the early years of this century. Judging by the photo, safety was not a big concern. The trees seem part of the fun and skiers converge at the bottom from all directions.

(Below centre) The Ottawa Ski Club, which would eventually become the largest in the world, was formed in 1910. The Rockcliffe escarpment was utilized by the club to hold the Canadian Ski Jumping Championships in 1914. As late as 1930, the event was still held here, with crowds thronging to watch the daredevil skiers fly through the air, coming to a stop near the river's edge.

(Below right) The Ottawa Ski Club would soon have more members than any other of its kind in the world. This was partially because the club ski hill was so accessible to Ottawans. Only a twenty-minute drive from the centre of Ottawa, Camp Fortune drew young and old to its exhilarating blend of outdoor thrills and social club atmosphere.

Downhill skiing has long been part of the fabric of growing up in Ottawa. There are many small, excellent ski slopes in the region, but the most familiar is the long running Camp Fortune, which was operated for many years by the Ottawa Ski Club. Today, the lifts are faster and the snow better, but the smiles are just the same. Like it or not, fashion has always been a part of the ski scene. In the early part of the century, these young Ottawa ladies (inset) were the height of femininity and post-Victorian charm. By the early 1990s, the art of skiing had been greatly advanced through boot and ski technology and fashions became more a statement of the joy inherent in the sport.

NATIONAL ARCHIVES OF CANADA / C-22150

NATIONAL ARCHIVE OF CANADA / PA-148970

CANADIAN SKI MUSEUM

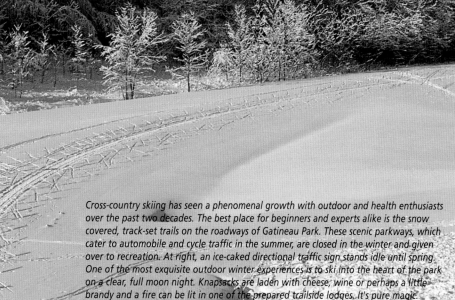

Cross-country skiing has seen a phenomenal growth with outdoor and health enthusiasts over the past two decades. The best place for beginners and experts alike is the snow covered, track-set trails on the roadways of Gatineau Park. These scenic parkways, which cater to automobile and cycle traffic in the summer, are closed in the winter and given over to recreation. At right, an ice-caked directional traffic sign stands idle until spring. One of the most exquisite outdoor winter experiences is to ski into the heart of the park on a clear, full moon night. Knapsacks are laden with cheese, wine or perhaps a little brandy and a fire can be lit in one of the prepared trailside lodges. It's pure magic.

The increase in cross-country activity has spawned enormous interest in ski racing. Today, there are several ski races in the area, none more grueling than the Keskinada Loppet, a 25-kilometer race from Val Tetreau, at the base of the Gatineau Parkway, up into the hills. The race attracts hundreds of expert skiers from around the region and even the world.

Today, Camp Fortune is one of four family-oriented ski resorts operating in the same neck of the Gatineau woods, all of which are within a half-hour of Ottawa.

It is often said that there are only two seasons in Ottawa – winter and four months of bad snowmobiling. For new Canadians, the first winter in Ottawa can be a bitter and depressing experience, especially if they come from sunnier climes. Some never get used to it, while others adjust. It's the next generation, one which was born into winter, that flourishes. The native-born citizens of Ottawa embrace the cold months, for they know there is much joy in its freeze. Others call it bitter; they call it crisp. Others see snow falling as a problem; they see snow falling as an opportunity for fun.

The biggest winter event in Ottawa is undoubtedly Winterlude, the celebration of our relationship with winter along the Rideau Canal. It is a time for even the most committed couch potato to lace up, to laugh and to feel the sun on the face and the ice underfoot. One thing strikes home when skating among the tens of thousands along the canal – everyone is smiling! An afternoon at Winterlude can include a tour of the snow sculptures on Dow's Lake, a leisurely skate to Fifth Avenue for the obligatory Beavertail pastry or to the National Arts Centre, if anyone is feeling really active. Along the way, skaters can enjoy outdoor figure skating demonstrations, food, and miles of the best natural ice in the world. NCC ice crews, well schooled in the science and art of ice making, prepare the canal afresh each night throughout the skating season.

Long before the 1970s opening of the world's longest skating rink, the canal was utilized for winter entertainment. In the 1950s, dogsled races were a popular event held on the frozen surface of the Rideau Canal. The Jack Snow Dog Derby course went from Union Station all the way to Dow's Lake and was lined with spectators. Today, dogsledding is still a popular part of Winterlude. The event takes place across the river at Jacques Cartier Park, at the Hull approach to the Interprovincial Bridge.

Hillary Rodham Clinton, First Lady of the United States, chats with Grant Hooker after tasting the "Killaloe Sunrise". Mr. Hooker, an American himself, created the quintessential Ottawa pastry over twenty years ago and today, no Ottawa family outing in winter is complete without one of his tasty concoctions.

116

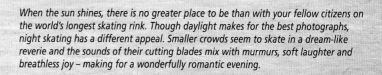

When the sun shines, there is no greater place to be than with your fellow citizens on the world's longest skating rink. Though daylight makes for the best photographs, night skating has a different appeal. Smaller crowds seem to skate in a dream-like reverie and the sounds of their cutting blades mix with murmurs, soft laughter and breathless joy – making for a wonderfully romantic evening.

During Winterlude, there are wonderful things for all ages to see and do, including ice-runner rides, snow and ice sculpting and the kids' favourite – the ice slides of Jacques Cartier Park.

SPARKS S^t.
APRIL

When the big blizzards of winter hit, the city barely misses a beat. Road crews, well aware of the coming storm are prepared. No matter how deep the accumulation, the city is always up and running by the next morning. The drivers of the region are some of the most experienced winter drivers this side of the prairies. In this photo of the eastbound Queensway at Bayshore Shopping Center, drivers give each other a wide berth to allow for any sudden stops.

Snow removal is a one of the fortes of Ottawa's municipal works crews. They are the Navy Seals of winter road clearing – disciplined, precise, quick and determined. Before the coming of the automobile (left inset), only the sidewalks were cleared. The snow was dumped in the middle of the street and horse drawn rollers flattened it for sleigh travel. Today, everything must go. In the two photos at left, we see a hundred years of snow removal tradition on Sparks Street.

Snow removal is an art learned from continued practice, and nowhere does anyone get more practice time than Ottawa. At left are three snow removal scenes of days gone by and at right are the modern day equivalents. In 1920 at the corner of Bank and Sparks Streets, road crews with a primitive conveyor feed snow to waiting dumptrucks. The open cabs of the tiny vehicles made this type of work a chilling experience. Today (right), huge snow removal teams, on the same spot, churn their way through a neat hedgerow of graded snow throwing it into the enormous boxes of multi-wheeled dumptrucks. These modern snowblowing machines could bury the old dumptrucks in seconds flat.

Snow removal has always been a team sport. In the 1920s, swarms of tiny underpowered wagons were necessary to get the snow out of the way of streetcar traffic on Preston Street. Today, coordinated teams of heavy, specialized machinery attack each street in turn in a choreographed ballet that shakes the neighbouring buildings to their foundations. Once the big snow has been taken off, trucks lay down a corrosive dosing of salt or brine and the street is vacated to let the combination of salt, traffic and sun to do its thing. The view at right is Cumberland Street near the Byward Market.

Today the big boys of snow removal are the insect-like graders. The old types were only for the toughest municipal employees, for it required that all the levers, wheels, chains and pedals be operated while standing on an open platform. The hard steel rubberless wheels could hardly have offered good purchase in light snow, let alone the kind of blankets that have been known to drop on the city each year. In the 1990s (right, Murray Street), graders offer unparalleled power and capability, while providing operators with the comforts of heat, air-ride seats and stereo music, but the work is still grueling and demanding. When the snow flies, the work cannot be delayed, so crews must labour hard until the job is done.

The Gatineau River, the third and equally important river along which Ottawa's history has coursed, flows down from the north out of Western Québec and joins the mighty Ottawa a mile east of Rideau Falls. It had been the conveyor of commerce for the Outaouais for many decades, as logs were floated downstream from upstream lumber camps, bound for the big CIP paper mill at Pointe Gatineau. The huge mill at the confluence of the Gatineau and Ottawa Rivers still dominates life and commerce in the sprawling community. Until only recently, the entire length of this fast moving river was choked with softwood logs. All along its banks and in the shallow fast moving sections, the logs were jammed like piles of giant pick-up-sticks. Throughout the logging season, crews were dispatched to free the revenue-generating wood from the morass (using gaffs and even dynamite) and send it on its way to be turned into newsprint paper for the great dailies of the American Northeast. Today, logs are trucked to the mill and the working river has been successfully returned to its natural state, much to the delight of the thousands of cottagers along its banks.

The photographs on these two pages show the same stretch of the Gatineau River near Ironside, Québec as it flows through four seasons. From spring's chaotic snowmelt to autumn's palette and even winter's foggy freeze, fast moving sections like this stay open all year round. In years past, the exposed rock would be jammed, sometimes to a great height, with the handiwork of upstream lumberjacks.

Much of the Gatineau River these days is lined with cottages, but in some respects this has had the benefit of limiting further development of the water's edge. Today, other than the lovely summertime residences, the river is much the same as when voyageurs rode the fast waters down to the Ottawa.

123

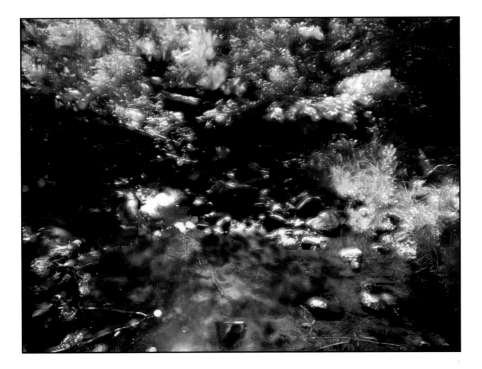

The Gatineau Hills are seamed with secret streams and waterfalls. A short hike from any road will bring you to a sun-dappled eddy or a rushing stream. Everywhere in the great rolling Gatineaus can be found hilltop lakes and pools. Their cold dark waters find outlet through rock face and creekbed. Water is part of the music of the old hills. In the deep clefts between the hills, it is a constant soundtrack, arranged by one greater than Handel, with the calls of woodland birds, the swish of the wind and the creak of boughs. It splashes and plays from rock to rock, sings mirthfully along stone beds, rushing and hissing as it picks up the river and is swept in the great cycle to the Ottawa and the St. Lawrence and the sea.

Magic Carpet Ride

The sun is barely over the horizon on a cool summer morning. Its rays stretch across the Nation's Capital, reaching at first for the tallest buildings, then the canyons between them. The tree-covered parkways have yet to feel the warmth, but sunlight outlines the silhouette of Parliament on the surface of the river and highlights the bridges and the early morning commuters.

VERY FEW OF US CAN REMEMBER A TIME BEFORE THERE WERE AIRPLANES. AND NO ONE HOLDING THIS BOOK WAS AROUND FOR THE INVENTION OF THE CAMERA. BUT OUR COMMUNITY HAS BEEN HERE FOR ALMOST 200 YEARS—IF WE TAKE THE BEGINNING OF WRIGHTSTOWN BY THAT TINY SETTLEMENT'S VISIONARY FOUNDER PHILEMON AS OUR STARTING POINT. SO, FOR THOSE EARLY YEARS, AERIAL PHOTOGRAPHY OF OUR TINY CORNER OF THE PLANET WAS IMPOSSIBLE. BUT THIS DIDN'T STOP THOSE FIRST SETTLERS FROM LOOKING UP AND IMAGINING WHAT THE BIRDS SOARING OVER THE FUTURE CAPITAL COULD SEE. AND A FEW OF THEM WERE SO INTRIGUED THEY LET THEIR IMAGINATION FLOW THROUGH PEN AND BRUSH TO PAPER, AND IT IS THROUGH THEIR EYES THAT WE WILL BEGIN OUR MAGIC CARPET RIDE OVER NEARLY TWO CENTURIES OF GROWTH.

126

CITY OF OTTAWA ⊙ CANADA WEST.

A favourite angle of photographers and of imagination since the days of Bytown has always been from around a thousand feet above and to the west of Parliament Hill. Of course, in this illustration from 1857, Parliament is only in the minds and on the drawing boards of its architects back in Great Britain. The great boiling cauldron of Chaudière, while bridged and lined with mills, is still not dammed.

The camera came along by the middle of the last century and our first aerial, photographic views of the emerging capital will be from a perch atop the old Victoria Tower on the original Parliament buildings, several years before Confederation. Following the Silver Dart, the Wright Brothers and the Great War, the Royal Canadian Air Force began aerial photography of Canada in earnest, and our first truly aerial photographic views date from the early 20's. So please fasten your seatbelts and enjoy the flight!

The "Westminster in the Wilderness" now lies complete, almost ten years after Confederation. The greatest development of the city stretches to the east in what was then called Lower Town. A forested Major's Hill climbs up from the river and cuts right to Sappers' Bridge, where new edifices and businesses have accumulated. At the east end of York Street and along the banks of the Rideau River rises a high hill; one that rises higher in the mind of the artist than it does in reality. Since the earliest artistic renderings of Bytown (see page 38), their creators have seen fit to increase geological activity to the east.

Climbing to two thousand feet, we see, one year later, that much has happened. Looking southeast, development now stretches in front of Parliament. Another bridge has spanned the canal to the south at Slater Street and the forest of Major's Hill has given way to manicured and landscaped parkland.

When one compares this image of Ottawa in 1926 with the modern one on the facing page, one is struck by the enormous changes that have occured in the last seven decades. Everything that we see, from Elgin Street east to the Canal, in this picture has now simply vanished. While many of these buildings were expropriated, many others were simply victims of fire. This was the case for the old City Hall, which can be seen in the treed area at the lower centre of this photo.

Open heart surgery. Great efforts were made throughout this century to develop the heart of Ottawa for all Canadians. In this modern view from a thousand feet over Somerset Street and looking north, we see the great swath of green space along both sides of the canal, Confederation Square, Confederation Park (centre), the National Arts Centre, and the War Memorial.
But they did not always exist. Rail lines cut to the heart of the city and industry blighted the canal in 1925 (left picture). By 1928 (centre) much of the blight has been cut away and structures along Confederation Square are being razed. Unfortunately, the Russell Hotel near the center of the square would have to be demolished after a fire. In 1945 (right), Confederation Square is the proud setting for the Cenotaph of the War Memorial. The very heart of Ottawa now beats proudly for those brave Canadians who gave their own hearts for the country they loved so much.

So much has changed even in the past few decades. Ottawa's downtown growth was hobbled for years by a well-intentioned bylaw that prevented development of any office buildings higher than the Peace Tower. Planners wanted sightlines to the tower from all angles to be uninterrupted. This in turn forced the too-quick destruction of many of our older buildings to make horizontal space for what should have been vertical development. In this 1960 photograph, we see the legislated dominance of Parliament over its surroundings. The train station and its tracks still slice through town and much of our precious space is occupied by "Temporary Buildings".

The bland clapboard expanses of the Temporary Buildings (Justice at bottom of picture and National Defence at upper right) marred the landscape of Ottawa for almost four decades. Built to house the brushfire expansion of government bureaucracy before and particularly during WWII, the buildings were always intended to be demolished just as soon as new, fully developed facilities could be mustered. The Temporary Building of National Defence came down in the '70s and is now the sight of Festival Plaza and the Headquarters of the Regional Municipality of Ottawa-Carleton.

(Upper right) In the 1980s, the former site of the E.B. Eddy pulpwood storage yards has been prepared for Douglas Cardinal's harmonious design for the Canadian Museum of Civilization, while across the river the land adjacent to Nepean Point awaits Moshe Safdie's brilliant National Gallery of Canada.

(Middle right) Height restrictions for development were modified in the 1970s and today, though the Peace Tower is hidden from the immediate south, things don't look all that bad. The parkway rolling into Ottawa along the river allows for all the spectacular view of Parliament and the city anyone could ever want and office workers can meter their importance to their companies or departments by the view of the Peace Tower they are allotted.

(Lower right) Though Ottawa and region boasts over a million citizens, a brisk walk of less than an hour will take one along Wellington, down Bay, east along Gloucester and up Elgin – the entire downtown core!

After this aerial tour of Ottawa then and now, we come full circle to where it all began – Chaudière Falls. When Champlain and his band of hearty men ventured up the river centuries ago, they most certainly heard the great falls long before they saw them and the water as they approached was surely foamed and swirling up from the depths. He could not have imagined what would come of this spot; how the waters would be tamed and almost beaten; how the encampment would grow into a village, into a town, into a city. He could not have known, as he stood tall in his canoe to survey the roaring torrent ahead, that he was standing at the very heart of one of the greatest nations on the planet. Then again maybe he did.

LEBRETON FLATS

HISTORY WAITING FOR THE FUTURE

The simple sketch above, by Colonel John By himself, shows the front elevation of Isaac Firth's Tavern, which was part of the first community on the south side of the river. This village, known as Richmond Landing, clung to the shoreline of what we now call Lebreton Flats and thrived due to its location next to the Chaudière Falls. The tavern, also called Mother Firth's, was built around 1809 to service passing voyageurs and raftsmen. It was located at the corner of present day Booth and Oregon Streets. Today, cars on the Western Parkway speed right past this historic old location without knowing that it all started here.

When the first Union Bridge was completed, it was not one span, but seven individual leaps across the boiling water. The southern most step in the construction was designed and executed in 1827 by one of By's junior engineering officers, Lt. Pooley. It traversed what was popularly known as "The Gulley". Colonel By was so impressed by the unique structure of the span, that he named it in Pooley's honour. Now it was possible for equipment and people to cross the river and this bridge was still in use in 1879 – the time of this painting. Though Pooley's Bridge stood the test of time, the larger Union Bridge span, buffeted by ice, collapsed into the "Big Kettle" in 1835. When its suspension bridge replacement was finally built in 1844, it was touted as one of the finest engineering feats in the land.

THE CAPITAL BY ANY OTHER NAME...

LIKE ANY AREA RICH IN HISTORY, THE CITY OF OTTAWA HAS CARRIED MANY IDENTITIES.

The local shoreline of the Ottawa River was first known as Nepean Point because of the township in which .it was located, named in honour of Sir Evan Nepean, British Secretary of State for Ireland. However, had Sir Evan's family name retained its original form, the township and the suburban city of Nepean would instead boast the title "Nanstean."

Later, the area was called Collins' Landing after the first person to build on the Ontario side of the river. Jehiel Collins was a United Empire Loyalist from Vermont who, in 1809, erected a log shanty tavern and store at the canoe landing below the Chaudière Falls to service the portage. He later sold out to his brother-in-law Caleb Bellows who improved the lot of river travellers by adding a wharf and, in return, the landing took on his name for a time.

It became known as Richmond Landing when the families of disbanded soldiers from the 99th Regiment of Foot camped on the river flats during the summer of 1819 while the soldiers hacked a 16-kilometre (10-mile) trail through the bush to the Jock River. There, they established the military town of Richmond and their bush trail is today called the Richmond Road, the oldest thoroughfare in Ottawa.

The area was also known variously as Iles aux Chaudières, Barrière, Chaudière Falls and even Rideau Canal. Finally, after 28 years as Bytown, the city of Ottawa made its debut on New Year's Day 1855, so named to commemorate the 200th anniversary of the opening of the river for peaceful navigation by the Outaouais Indians and their French allies, after years of war between them and the Iroquois-English alliance.

Though Chaudière Falls, Richmond Landing and Lebreton Flats were the original location of town growth, they remain today, the largest undeveloped piece of property in the city. Lebreton Flats, though wiped off the map in the Great Fire of 1900, rebounded quickly. By the 1960s, its post-fire growth was starting to deteriorate into urban blight. The flat land (top), looking west, housed lower income housing and industrial sites, which planners hoped to eradicate because of their proximity to Upper Town and the nation's seat of government. The building at lower right is the old Water Works, still in use today to provide Upper Town with water.

By the mid-1960s (centre), the bulldozers were doing their stuff as the homes of many of Ottawa's working class people had disappeared. The industry and rail lines were soon to follow. In this view looking east, we see that the midstream island known as Victoria Island (upper left corner) is covered in WWII era temporary buildings still in the employ of the Defence Construction agency of DND.

Looking northwest today, we see that the land has not yet found an appropriate use, kept vacant by the National Capital Commission. Though many citizens want it to be put to use, the planners of the Commission have rightly waited for some greater purpose. From high above we can see that the road plan remains and though there are no homes or businesses, the municipal street signs still exist at each corner.

UPPER TOWN
GROWING UP NEXT TO PARLIAMENT

When we decide to build a new office building today, we think in terms of an entire city block. Take down what ever was there, drop the parking five stories below and reach for the skies. But it was not always like that.
At the turn of the century in Upper Town Ottawa, each city block was lined on all four sides with three-, four- and five-storey buildings from thirty to 100 feet wide. Each was elegant in its own way, with arched windows, ornate masonry, expansive fascia and discreet entrances. The detail and scale of the environment of those unenlightened years was what the enlightened planners of today try so vainly to achieve. The streets of Ottawa, though especially wide by design of Colonel By himself, were great accumulators of snow in winter. As today, the streets and sidewalks had to be cleared immediately or commerce and life would grind to a frozen standstill. Horsedrawn wagons and muscle power were employed, where today blowers, graders and dumptrucks are used. The job was excruciatingly slow and backbreaking, but it had to be done. In this picture, taken mid-storm on Sparks Street in the winter of 1891, city works crews take a moment from their labour to pose for the photographer.

It took many people to make a city work in the 19th century. In addition to hand-removed snow, water was drawn from the river by horse and distributed around town in barrels. The driver of this "puncheon" makes his way uptown, despite the driving winter storm, to sell his 25 cents-a-barrel winter water (15 cents for the summer variety). The water, though deemed clean enough to drink, was full of impurities and was the eau-de-source of typhoid and other diseases. It wasn't until 1875 that the first tap water was made available to Ottawa households from the new pumping station at the Water Works. The Water Works, located at the edge of Lebreton Flats, near the western end of Queen Street, still pumps much of the water used by Upper Town to this day.

A PARADOX OF HISTORY

NATIONAL ARCHIVES OF CANADA / 041323

CITY OF OTTAWA ARCHIVES / CA-19070

"A TRIP ON THE BACKBONE OF AN EARTHQUAKE," IS HOW ONE OTTAWA BUSINESSMAN DESCRIBED A DRIVE ALONG SPARKS STREET IN 1895.

That July, however, the three blocks between Elgin and Bank streets were transformed by the first sheet of asphalt to be laid in the National Capital and the new surface was "subjected to tests from canes and umbrella points" by an appreciative crowd of more than 300 citizens drawn to witness the event.

In 1891, the Ottawa Electric Railway Company had been awarded a 20 year charter to operate the city's first horseless streetcars, three of which were fitted two years later with 500-volt heaters, making them the first electrically heated streetcars in the world. In spite of this competitive edge, however, it was the horse-drawn trams of the Ottawa City Passenger Railway that still controlled the best routes in town, including Sparks Street.

By the end of the 19th century, Sparks had become the "Broadway" of Ottawa, with a profusion of power, telephone, telegraph and tram wires, five- and six-storey highrises and constant traffic. It was already a far cry from that summer day five years earlier when first, according to The Ottawa Citizen, "bicyclists gazed on the enticing surface and smiled in sweet contentment."

It is a paradox of history that the very first street paved in the capital to smooth the way for vehicles would, in 1960, become Canada's very first mall restricted to pedestrians only.

The short two blocks along Elgin Street from Wellington to Queen have seen endless change, razing and rebuilding over the past century - probably more than any other part of Ottawa. In 1865, as Canada was gearing up for nationhood, the street was dirt, the sidewalk wood. At the corner stood the Russell House tavern and hotel and a general store – hardly the thing you would expect in the very shadow of the almost finished Parliament Buildings. Across the street were more buildings of the same type on the future site of the National War Memorial.

Ten years later, where once stood a confectioner, the northwest corner of Elgin and Sparks now boasts a more substantial building housing a wholesaler. In the earliest days of the capital, fire was the greatest urban renewer. If a fire didn't sweep away the whole neighbourhood, it could be counted on to gut a few buildings before it could be controlled. The Russell House, for instance (top photo), was razed by fire and rebuilt across the street as the magnificent Russell Hotel which in turn burned to the ground in 1928.

After the Changing the Guard Ceremony on Parliament Hill, the Ceremonial Band, with instruments silent, make their way south to the Cartier Square Drill Hall. The great sweeping vista of Confederation Square, or "Confusion Square" as Ottawans like to call it, takes in the East Block of Parliament, the War Memorial, the Chateau Laurier, Union Station and the National Arts Centre and all the bridgework and landscaping that connect them. We have come to view the Elgin streetscape as wide open and sunlit, but in 1875 it was as narrow a street as there was to be found in the new Capital, with lowrise buildings of stone or wood running both sides of its entire length.

In 1867, Ottawa was entering the international stage as the capital of a new and vast country. The fabulous Parliament Buildings, designed by architect Thomas Fuller, now dominate the uptown scene and, by comparison, all else looks shabby. This view, up Elgin to the East Block, shows how buildings reached north, right up to the edge of the Hill.

By 1898, much of the forlorn lowrise structures on Elgin, within the first few blocks of Wellington, have been replaced. The newly finished East Gate opens up to a more appropriate scene of Victorian and Italian Romanesque (sometimes jokingly referred to as "Russian Gothic") buildings like the ten-year old Langevin Block (right). The Langevin Block (also designed by Thomas Fuller) was originally intended as the "Southern Block" of the Parliament Buildings.

Today, the east side of Elgin Street remains open, allowing sunlight to fill the square. The old Victorian Post Office (on the present day site of the War Memorial) was demolished only five decades after its construction and was rebuilt at its present location at the corner of Sparks Street. The corner of Sparks and Elgin has long been considered the gateway to Upper Town and its commercial and government offices.

Sparks Street has long been the nucleus of Ottawa's uptown commerce. The land beneath was purchased by Irish immigrant Nicholas Sparks (the namesake of Nicholas Street as well) from John Burrows, five years before the coming of Colonel By. After the construction of the Parliament Buildings, development of Sparks' former land accelerated, putting Sparks Street at the very centre of activity. Looking down Sparks Street in the early 1900s from the present site of the War Memorial, activity and bustle is everywhere. Electric streetcars line the roadway in a scene reminiscent of today's OC Transpo bus malls.

In the first decade of the 20th century, Sparks Street was the epitome of industrious commercial activity. Looking west along the street from Metcalfe, we see that the city is making good use of modern inventions such as electric lights, electric streetcars and telephone and telegraph. The clatter and screech of streetcars and clop of hooves most certainly would have made for a cacophonous stroll, but the excitement of the city's undeniable growth was also in the air.

A century later, good planning intentions and millions of dollars of development funds have reduced the importance of the Sparks Street Mall to a shadow of what it once was. In the late '60s and '70s, before the advent of mega-shopping centres like the Rideau Centre, the pedestrian mall concept was so successful that Sparks Street merchants were among the busiest in the city. Today, though efforts are still being made to renew commerce on the street, stores continue to close. On a stormy Sunday in winter, pedestrians are as rare as passenger pigeons.

For a street that saw the first automobile an Ottawa, it is ironic that it would eventually become a permanent pedestrian mall. The first design concept for the mall was an international benchmark in town planning and garnered much attention worldwide. Crowds came to stroll the mall at lunchtime, to shop, to see and to be seen. Waterfalls, street performers, Hari Krishna monks and comfortable benches made "The Mall" the "coolest" place to be in the city. Today, though millions have been spent to upgrade the mall's urban architecture, its pedestrian lifeblood continues to dwindle.

The corner of Sparks and Metcalfe Streets has long felt the pulse of a great nation. In 1916, (inset) a look north from Sparks would have shown the devastation wrought by the fire of the previous winter. Looking past the Rideau Club on the left (itself a victim of fire in the late 1970s), we see straight to the Library, which survived the conflagration. The scene today (above) still has the same buildings, but the Centre Block has been rebuilt and now the Rideau Club, where Ottawa's male elite convened for a century, has succumbed.

Where did everyone go when Victory in Europe was announced? Straight to Parliament Hill and then to Sparks Street for a noisy and littered parade, that's where. Ottawans, elated that the hardships of the past six years have come to an end and hopeful for the return of their sons, gather together at the corner of Sparks and Metcalfe to let off some steam. The building at the corner still exists today, the home of a long-standing tourist boutique aptly named Canada's Four Corners. In 1999, at the turn of yet another century, Metcalfe and Sparks Street remain important crossroads for Ottawa's future development.

141

(Top left) O'Connor Street grew as long as Bytown and Ottawa saw development. The street was named after Daniel O'Connor, one of Ottawa's early pillars of society, and a local magistrate. Today, it stretches as far south as Monkland Avenue in the area known as the Glebe, but at the outset, it was but a few blocks long. Looking from atop the West Block tower, we see that, after a few dirt covered blocks, urban Ottawa peters out to farmland.

(Lower left) Looking north now, in the winter of 1880, Ottawa, and in particular O'Connor Street, has seen tremendous development. In the distance, the Mackenzie Tower of the West Block stands high above O'Connor's new buildings.

(Above) Early city fathers would have a hard time recognizing O'Connor Street today. The construction of mega-office complexes in the 1980s wiped out much of what was still left of O'Connor's oldest buildings, including the historic Bytown Inn at the corner of Albert Street. O'Connor has become a glass canyon, where some of Ottawa's most prestigious and expensive offices are located.

Ottawa's most important north-south arterial is Bank Street. Where it intersects Sparks Street, once Ottawa's busiest commercial district, was in days gone by, a great place to set up shop. Important intersections usually create heavy traffic and it was no different in 1912 (above), as we look west across Bank Street. Electric streetcars vie for right of way with horse drawn carts, while pedestrians jay walk with impunity since slow moving carts and trams were easy to avoid. Today, (top left) the electric lines, poles and streetcar wires are gone, but so is much of the excitement. Looking north past the rounded facade of the Sun Life (Mercury) Building to the elegant but stodgy Metropolitan Life Building, it is noted that at least the east side of Bank Street has escaped the wreckers ball. Actually, the most beautiful part of the Sun Life Building (bottom left, early 1900s) was lopped off – the ornate domed cupola featuring a statue of Mercury, Roman god of commerce. But thankfully it was retained, restored and relocated atop the Mercury Court building in the Byward Market. On a snowy Sunday morning in 1999 (below), a truncated remnant of the Mercury Building awaits the sunshine and the arrival of weekday shoppers.

In 1853, when this painting of the corner of Bank and Wellington Streets was created, the British Government realized that the United States no longer posed a threat. In that year, they handed over the management of the canal system to the government of Canada West (as it was called then) for use as a commercial waterway. British Army presence was withdrawn and the military hospital on Barracks Hill would soon make way for the foundation work of the new Houses of Parliament. 150 years ago, the area immediately west of Barracks Hill was the nucleus of westward development. Where working class homes and businesses first stood, an enclave of some of Ottawa's most well to do families was born. It did not last long, and homes, which were not destroyed in the Great Fire of 1900, were expropriated. Today and forever, it is the site of our law making. Construction of the Confederation Building (far right), home of many Members of Parliament was commenced here in 1928, the Justice Building (centre) in 1935 and the Supreme Court (left and inset) in 1938. The tiny yet spectacular park and lookout behind the Supreme Court is one of the best kept secrets in all Ottawa.

The passing parade of time is always intriguing for those who know what to look for. Close inspection of yet another "old picture" of Ottawa reveals much. In 1870, the grounds of Parliament Hill remain under construction, three years after the opening of Parliament. From the edge of the plateau occupied by the West Block, we gaze over the debris of construction upon an expanding Upper Town. A hundred yards east of Bank, St. Andrew's Presbyterian Church stands ready to receive its new steeple. The original St. Andrew's (the first stone church in Bytown) was constructed on this spot in 1828 by Scottish masons who worked in their spare time. Such was the power and commercial dominance of the Scottish lumber and land barons, that the church could be demolished and replaced with a more imposing one in only fifty years.

At the very edge of the Hill, amidst the rubble and muck, stand the newly completed wall and West Gate, made of freshly quarried sandstone cut from the bedrock of Nepean, some 12 miles west. In the early 1900s (lower right), magnificent trees have taken over along the edge of Parliament and shade the stone wall on a hot summer afternoon. It will not be for some years, but the buildings beneath the Mackenzie Tower will be demolished and the land applied to more federal pursuits. Either electric streetcars were more ubiquitous in those days than OC Transpo buses are today, or photographers waited for their passage, for nearly every photograph taken in this period shows streets choked with the squealing beasts.

Both the gates to Parliament Hill and the steeple of St. Andrew's are all that is to be seen today (bottom left) of the buildings and homes photographed above. Wellington, though undergoing continuous construction for over a hundred years still retains its air of importance, enhanced perhaps by its proximity to Canada's most important piece of real estate. The gates, now darkened by airborne pollution, still remain open for any Canadian wishing to stroll the grounds of their Parliament.

Many of Ottawa's sublime parks were not always the haunts of sun worshipping civil servants and raucous school children on fieldtrips. Most were wrested from earlier developments as land was expropriated for the future use of all citizens. When Bytown was young, there was no need of green open spaces, since a short walk in any direction would lead into the wilderness itself. But soon, as the city matured, it became necessary to take back some of the land for the purposes of peace of mind. Confederation Park, which temporarily occupied the land north of the National Arts Centre, lies now between the approaches to MacKenzie-King and Laurier Bridges.

The historic granite water fountain, which delights and cools a young mother and her child, was once splashing at the centre of London's Piccadilly Circus. In the background stands the Lord Elgin Hotel, one of only two grand hotels remaining which predate WWII.

From the front door of the Lord Elgin Hotel in 1928 we see not open common space but small business and the Roxborough Apartments. Nearly all of Ottawa's exquisite parks were retaken from less meditative uses. The breathtaking bikeway (upper right), which follows the edge of the Ottawa River below Parliament Hill, was once lined with logs; the Rideau Canal itself (centre) was a busy waterway despoiled by commerce and Commissioner's Park on the shore of Dow's Lake was an unsightly lumberyard just 75 years ago.

CITY OF OTTAWA ARCHIVES / CA-19907

NATIONAL ARCHIVES OF CANADA / PA-131639

Today, the Headquarters of the Regional Municipality of Ottawa-Carleton is located in a post-modern building on Lisgar Street. The new structure is also connected to a renovated Gothic Revival structure (upper left and inset), which once housed the Ottawa Teachers College (sometimes called the Ottawa Normal School). Not too long ago, it was engaged in the education of Ottawa's first rate teaching professionals, as it had done since 1875. In the winter of 1895 (lower left), it was a modern and respected centre of advanced learning (one of only two in Ontario) for what was then, as now, a very respected profession. Mature hardwoods shaded the grounds on the south lawn of the building as they continue to do today. The tall limbless trees connected by wires have long since vanished. In 1909, aspiring teachers (lower right) were expected to tend to the flower gardens surrounding the Normal School, ostensibly to learn about botany, but also to keep ground maintenance costs to a minimum. These gardens were located at the east end of the college, where today a cobblestone courtyard (upper right) functions just as well to keep maintenance costs to a minimum.

Lisgar Collegiate was Ottawa's first secondary school, but it was not always graduating students from its present location. First established in 1843, when rough and raucous Bytown was little more than the Tombstone of the North, the school we now know as Lisgar Collegiate leased its premises at various locations. It wasn't until 1874 that it found a permanent home along the Rideau Canal. The school was destroyed by fire in 1893, rebuilt the next year and enlarged again in 1902. Today, a much larger Lisgar Collegiate still has a reputation of the highest standard, attracting students from the entire city. Its proximity to the Rideau Canal entices students to make use of the shade and cool grass along the Queen Elizabeth Driveway, where they relax and study.

In 1904, well-to-do parents had their drivers drop their teenagers off at the newly enlarged Lisgar Collegiate. Times have not changed much after all, for today, upscale parents from the trendy downtown neighbourhoods still chauffeur their sons and daughters – but in the family Sport Utility Vehicle.

The site of present day Lansdowne Park was chosen as far back as 1874, for exhibitions and, in 1879, it was the location for the Great Dominion Exhibition. Folks questioned the choice, which they felt was too far out of town. Despite this perceived distance, the fields soon became the permanent location for a yearly regional exhibition. The Central Canada Exhibition was inaugurated in 1888 and soon became one of the premier agricultural and manufacturing fairs in all North America.

In 1925 (above), Lansdowne Park was much different than it is today. From the air, we can see the football field overlaid with a baseball diamond and surrounded by a horse racing track. A group of shed-roofed buildings to the south are intriguing – perhaps they are stables for the track. The beautiful scenic driveways on both sides of the canal, which we have come to love, are yet to be constructed in this photo.

For over a century, the Central Canada Exhibition has remained the most exciting event held in the city during the summer. From the outset, the "Ex" was meant to provide all citizens with a demonstration of our progress and production, a statement of where we stood as a community and a gauge for all to measure our growth. Included in the concept has always been a degree of thrills, slack-jawed voyeurism and willing submission to hucksterism. Back in the 1950s the original concept was still going strong (upper right). A mixture of side shows, midway rides, bandshell concerts and agricultural showcases drew folks from a radius of over 100 miles. In the 1950s there were still many mature trees throughout Lansdowne Park under which families would relax. A curving main street of side shows and burlesque tents featured such eye-popping delights as the Coppertone Review, The Wall of Death, Indigo Man, Lobster Boy or the Giant Rats of Sumatra. Children stared at the garish painted canvas tents and gripped their fathers hands tightly; delighted screams rose from the midway; the Vegamatic man held them spellbound and Red Skelton had them laughing in the aisles of the grandstand. The smells of hay and manure mixed with those of grilled sausage and popcorn in a heady intoxicating atmosphere.

The Aberdeen Pavilion, long the centrepiece of Lansdowne Park, has been an exhibition hall, Stanley Cup venue, military encampment, animal barn, broomball rink and even a movie studio. Threatened with demolition after years of neglect, it became the subject of heated debate in the early 1990s. Heritage-minded citizens won out over fiscal conservatives and the Aberdeen Pavilion (known by locals as the "Cattle Castle"), was completely restored to its 1903 grandeur (right).

Today, a much diminished "Super Ex" still draws hundreds of thousands, but gone are the grandstand shows and agricultural and community exhibits. Today Ottawans and folks from around the region still enjoy the midway although commercial displays have replaced those of the community. The Aberdeen Pavilion still enjoys a prominent place, but the grandstand remains largely unused.

The Ottawa Rough Riders of the CFL were a part of city life for nearly a century. Though money issues and modern business styles have thrust them completely into the realm of history, they were once the greatest team in all of Canada. Throughout the 1960s and 1970s the "'Riders" dominated the league and won several Grey Cups. The names say it all: Frank Clair, Bobby Simpson, Russ Jackson, Ron Stewart, Whit Tucker and Tony Gabriel. In this evening football game in the 1960s, we see the landmark forty-foot hedge of Lombardy poplars that once shielded neighbouring streets from the always active venue.

The former "Smyth Road Woods" is now the site of "Hospital Row", a complex of four different hospitals. The Perley and Rideau Veterans Centre (in distance at top) is an ultramodern medical and long-term care facility dedicated to Canada's military veterans. The Children's Hospital of Eastern Ontario (top centre), a world-class facility, specializes in the welfare of kids from the entire region and beyond. The Ottawa General Hospital (center), a teaching hospital affiliated with the University of Ottawa, moved here in the 1980s from its former site in Lower Town. The National Defence Medical Centre, which offers first class care to the Canadian military and their families (left) was the first major hospital to be constructed in the area. In the 1960s, when NDMC was under construction (inset), the rambling bungalows of the Rideau Veterans Home (upper right of inset) still housed disabled veterans of both world wars.

Seen here (left) under construction a year before, the Civic Hospital (now called the Civic Campus of the Ottawa Hospital) was completed in 1924. For several years, it was nicknamed "Fisher's Folly" after Mayor Harold Fisher, who campaigned vigourously for its construction after a particularly deadly influenza epidemic swept the city in 1917. It was considered folly because people thought it was too far from town. Today a statue of Mayor Fisher, commemorating his foresight, stands in front of the hospital's main building, but 75 years later, the Civic continues to weather controversy and the surgical knife of cost-efficiency. The expanded hospital facility (above) also includes the world famous Loeb Research Institute and the University of Ottawa Heart Institute. The large white cross on the south side of Carling Avenue marks a helipad for emergency transfer of patients.

QUEENSWAY
ONCE DIVIDED, NOW CONNECTED

Starting in 1957, and continuing in stages until 1965, Ottawa constructed a 17-mile limited access, multi-lane freeway known as the Queensway on the old Canada-Atlantic railbed which cut from east to west. As each stretch of rail was reclaimed, the new freeway grew until its completion. Today, the Queensway is considerably longer, stretching across the region from Stittsville in the west to Orleans in the east. In 1957 (left), the effect of rail lines and spurs ripping the city in two can be seen. The same scene today looking west from the Rideau Canal (inset lower left), shows how the Queensway has made good use of industrial property to join the city together, alleviating pressures on other arterials.

Two of the largest interchanges in the system are St. Laurent Boulevard (above), where we see the huge expanse of the St. Laurent Shopping Centre, and Alta Vista (below). At Alta Vista interchange, we see where the train station and post office were relocated (left) to allow for development of a more cohesive city. Also at this busy intersection, we can see Jetform Stadium, home of the Triple A Ottawa Lynx, and the Headquarters of the RCMP at the bend in the river.

CITY OF OTTAWA ARCHIVES/CA-8253

For decades, the railway tracks which sliced through the city, from north to south and from east to west, had curtailed serious development. In particular, the east-west rail line virtually cut the city in half (above).

154

The area at Nicholas Street (above), where the rail lines cut north, was particularly difficult to deal with during construction. In 1960, the highly industrialized wasteland included rail yards, city maintenance yards, gasworks, roundhouse and lines running to Union Station. These facilities could not simply be cut off, since all were still functioning. Clearly completed at this time however, is the multi-lane spans at old Hurdman Bridge, which were ready to receive the new divided highway. In the identical picture, taken 40 years later (above right), the old city yard at Hurdman Bridge is the only remaining industrial function.

Looking west from above the present day site of Jetform Park, we see the Alta Vista interchange well underway in the 1960s. The RCMP has just moved their headquarters into the big white building, which was originally built as a seminary. Note the fan of bridges crossing the river – two train trestles to the right, the new Queensway bridge, the old Hurdman Bridge and another train trestle to the north. Today (lower right), only one trestle remains and the old Hurdman Bridge is gone. The remaining trestle is now used as part of the city's myriad cycle paths.

We see now that everything has been cleaned up for a number of years. Large apartments have arisen at the intersection and a modern rapid transit system cuts a channel from downtown to cross the river. The former Ottawa Gasworks land is now the site of a campus of Algonquin College, formerly the Eastern Ontario Institute of Technology (upper right in photo), Ottawa's first community college.

BRITANNIA
HEAVEN ON THE OUTSKIRTS OF TOWN

The Britannia Yacht Club, a.k.a. Britannia Aquatic Club, Britannia Nautical Club and Britannia Boating Club, was first established in 1887 to promote the sports of sailing and paddling. Its first Regatta Day was held in 1891 and, as a boating event, is still held to this day. In 1898, Ottawans, who enjoy the outdoors, crowd the verandah and lakeside to catch the action. Today, it boasts many members, whose white-sailed boats dot the great expanse of Britannia Bay throughout the summer. The Ottawa River, west of the Des Chênes Rapids, widens greatly to form a body of water known as Lac Des Chênes. Because of its size and proximity to town, the lake is Ottawa's favourite sailing water. From here, sailboats and motorcraft can navigate far upstream.

At the end of another gorgeous day, a yachtsman enjoys a relaxing moment beneath the mast and yard.

This vivid painting captures the elements that make sailing at the BYC so addictive – open sky, steady winds and the elegance of club life.

From high above the BYC (above), we see the walled channel that leads to the basin and the boat slips. Below, a day sailor makes port under power, at the end of yet another perfect day.

For the citizens of Ottawa, who were not wealthy enough to belong to the elite yacht club, Britannia Bay had much to offer at the turn of the century. For those seeking relief from summer's swelter, there was always the streetcar ride (lower left) out to Britannia-on-the-Bay, where one could stroll the cool, wind swept pier out to the boathouse (upper left). Here a sun-shaded steamboat awaited to take the overdressed recreationists over the lake and up the Ottawa. Those who could not afford the tour, could take in the sights from the edge of the pier (centre left) or relax at the two magnificent pavilions at the water's edge. The pier is no longer there, but a stone breakwater now reaches out in the same spot. The streetcar ride was one of the most exciting events for children in these early years. In an era before the doubtful benefits of video games, television and walkmans, the simple pleasures of a clanging streetcar and the adventure of a summer outing in grand style had a powerful effect on the heart. Britannia today is still a beautiful place, however it is more a west end community park than all Ottawa's.

IN MEMORY

On the eleventh hour of the eleventh day of the eleventh month, Canadians everywhere bow their heads in a minute of silence for the sacrifices made by veterans of the Boer War,

CITY OF OTTAWA ARCHIVES / CA-0200

The ice draped statue of Colonel Gough (top left). the first commanding officer of the Princess Patricia's Canadian Light Infantry, looks out over the spot where, in 1914, his unit marched off to war. In an emotional and patriotic parade, the newly formed "Princess Pats" marched from their marshalling camp at Lansdowne Park (above) to board troop trains at Union Station. In 1919 (below), after five years of brutal and senseless conflict, the highly-decorated and war-weary Princess Pats stand to attention in front of Union Station to take the salute of the Canadian people. Today all veterans who made the ultimate sacrifice are remembered on the same spot.

NATIONAL ARCHIVES OF CANADA / PA-99796

The faces of Canada's proud WWII veterans and those of the mothers of fallen soldiers are powerful

WWI, WWII and the Korean War. The national television broadcast of the Remembrance Day Ceremony takes place at the National War Memorial on Confederation Square.

CITY OF OTTAWA ARCHIVES / CA-18238

CITY OF OTTAWA ARCHIVES / CA-18626

Construction of the National War Memorial was championed by Prime Minister King to pay homage to the 50,000 Canadians who were killed in WWI. It was well underway in 1938 (above) and soon ready for the spectacular and moving 1939 unveiling (below) by King George VI and Queen Elizabeth (today's Queen Mother) on the very eve of yet another horrific world war. The inescapable power and emotion of the Cenotaph was the work of Sydney and Vernon March (one is posing with three of the figures at left) and features 23 soldiers, sailors, airmen, medics and nurses.

and poignant reminders of what we normally take for granted – our freedom. God bless them all.

CITY OF OTTAWA ARCHIVES / CA-19080

As Ottawa is the Nation's Capital, its citizens are blessed with many spectacles on or above Parliament Hill. Twice a year, during the National Capital Air Show and on Canada Day, the skies over Ottawa are the stage for a patriotic and heart-pounding flypast of Canada's Snowbirds. 431 Air Demonstration Squadron, the Snowbirds, who will be entering their 30th year of operations in 2000, overfly the new Embassy of the United States inbound for Parliament Hill. The nine-plane formation headed by Team Lead, Major Bob Painchaud offers up this salute to the men and women of the Canadian Air Force, which is celebrating its 75th Anniversary in 1999. In addition, the Snowbirds pay tribute to "Team Aviano", whose members are presently risking their lives as part Canada's contribution to Operation 'Allied Force' in Yugoslavia.

The soldiers who did not come home after the "War to End All Wars" faced much misery and hardship before they died. That is why the War Memorial, for those who take the opportunity to look, is even more poignant in grey, rainy weather or when covered with a frozen mantle.

160

The red maple leaf snaps in the wind, as Canadian Forces CF-18 Hornet fighter aircraft of the "Desert Cats" composite air unit execute a hard break over Canadian Forces Base Uplands in 1991. They are returning from operations in the Gulf War, where they provided combat air patrols and close air support as part of the allied United Nations effort. These were the first Canadian aircraft to fly into combat since V-E Day.

Peacemaking and peacekeeping are fortes of the soldiers, airmen and sailors of the Canadian Forces. Since Lester B. Pearson won the Nobel Peace Prize for the conception of the UN peacekeeping force, Canadian soldiers have honoured our country by participating in every effort.

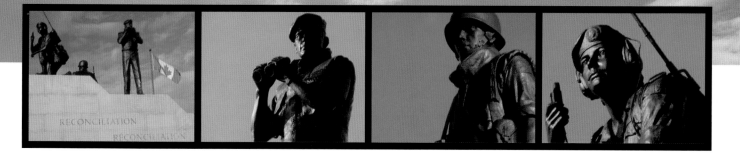

The Peacekeeping Memorial commemorates not war and the ultimate sacrifice, but honour and reason in a chaotic world. The bronze figures of three Canadian soldiers stand atop the ruins of war, ever vigilant against human folly and anger.

1860   1872   1892

CA. 1900   CA. 1920   CA. 1930

From a vantagepoint atop the Parliament Buildings, we watch as the heart of the Nation's Capital grows and changes with the times. In 1860, shortly after the building of Parliament was commenced, construction debris litters the eastern edge of old Barracks Hill. In the background stands the single span of Sappers' Bridge, the first to reach across the canal, connecting Upper and Lower Towns. In 1872, crews labour to complete a parallel span called Dufferin Bridge. Again in 1892, development east of the canal intensifies around Rideau Street and we see a well manicured park at Major's Hill, where the Chateau Laurier Hotel would soon exist.

In 1900, Ottawa faced an exciting and new century much the same as we do now. Development is furious and the west end of the bridges shows remarkable growth, with Victorian structures crowding the edge of Elgin from both sides. The large boat-turning basin that occupied the east bank has been partially filled in, signalling the end of the canal's commercial viability. As further proof of this condition, rail lines have now reached along the canal's edge to Sappers' Bridge. The large military parade ground, known as Cartier Square, can be seen in the distance. The drill hall at its eastern end still exists today as the starting off point for the daily Changing the Guard Ceremony. By 1920, things are moving fast for the heart of Ottawa. Twenty years has seen the construction of Union Station and the Chateau Laurier Hotel and Upper Town is booming. While Ottawans are familiar with the automobile, much of downtown traffic is still of the horse drawn variety. By 1930, things seem to be reversing. Gone already is the Russell Hotel and Confederation Park has been reclaimed from its site. It's only a matter of a few years before the Post Office is demolished to make way for the War Memorial. In the distance at right, stands the old Ottawa City Hall. The hoot of train whistles and the honk of automobile horns have now almost completely replaced the sound of hooves as the new city sound. Today (left), things still have not stabilized, as construction is underway to revitalize Plaza Bridge, which was created by the joining of the Sappers' and Dufferin Bridges.

Around 1890, visitors at the top of the Victoria Tower looked out upon a capital city, which had not yet fully matured. Buildings along Canada's most important stretch of roadway were still inconsequential, with rough looking sheds filling in some of the gaps. The newly constructed "Southern" or Langevin Block is the only edifice worthy of the "Federal" adjective. Today Wellington Street, though stately, still remains largely an underutilized property, ripe for some future plan. On a bleak winter morning, planners hidden from view in some Public Works office still contemplate its glorious future.

The four-year old Dufferin Bridge (right) alleviates much of the traffic problems that congested the old Sappers' Bridge (left). Joining Rideau and Wellington Streets into one long avenue, Dufferin creates a small triangular island between the two bridges, where, within two years (1875), the Post office was erected. In 1877, horse drawn omnibuses are the public transport of the day and, in the distance on Sparks Street, we see the offices of the Ottawa Citizen.

A quarter of a century later, things are much the same, but now electric streetcars are the technology de jour and horse drawn wagons and carriages have learned to share the road. A covered stairway leads down from Sappers' Bridge to the edge of the canal, where a train car awaits both passengers and the coming of Union Station.

In 1911, the scene at Dufferin Bridge is one of incredible bustle. The tall steel framework of the new Chateau Laurier Hotel rises above the bridge, while across the street (not in picture), the new Union Station is also under construction. Ottawans, as they have done since By's era, lean against the bridge rail to watch a canal bulk carrier enter the last lock on its way up from Entrance Bay. Its empty holds lead to conjecture that the boat has just made delivery of yellow sulphur to the pulp mills below the locks.

By 1925, horses had been replaced by horsepower and parking was obviously just as problematic then as it is today. The original Sappers' and Dufferin Bridges were demolished in 1912 to make way for a new plaza called Connaught Place. Though much the same in span and width as the twin bridges, the new Plaza Bridge was as much as fifteen feet lower. This can be seen by looking at the Post Office, which has magically sprouted another floor (the exposed basement).

In 1930, much of the Elgin-Wellington-Sparks triangle has been reclaimed for the city. Confederation Park (left) now stands where the old Russell Hotel and stage theatre once stood. Only the Post Office remains, but its days are numbered. In 1938, it too would come down and the operation moved across Elgin to its present location at the northwest corner of Sparks. The Central Chambers Building, at the corner of Queen and Elgin, one of Ottawa's best examples of early office architecture, can be seen in both photos.

Development of the bridges over the Rideau Canal is ongoing to this day. In 1998, they remained much the same as when work was being completed for the new Confederation Square and War Memorial. A comparison of the 1998 photo above and one from 1938 (far left), reveals almost identical hoarding, construction yards, sheds and debris. Scaffolding (upper right) surrounds the early stages of the granite work on the new Cenotaph. The latest plan will lead to partially separating the two former spans, this time to allow light and tourists to reach the canal beneath. Jackhammers add to the traffic chaos at "Confusion Square", as construction workers push hard to complete the latest iteration of the bridge in time for the spectacular celebrations slated for Parliament Hill at the beginning of the new millennium.

Storm clouds have cleared out from the west, enough to allow the setting sun to bathe the Alexandra Bridge in a sparkling golden hue, made all the more beautiful by the looming storm clouds behind. The Alexandra, or Interprovincial Bridge, today provides pedestrians with the most magnificent panorama Ottawa has to offer.

A setting sun, on yet another perfect evening, accentuates the details at the edge of the still waters. Viewed from the former Fitzgibbon's Landing below the bridge, the bullnose casements of the lower lock catch the same sun which highlights both tour boat and Parliamentary tower. Aware that many cyclists and pedestrians would stop to take in the formidable view, the NCC has constructed a number of well-appointed overlooks (left inset), where people can rest and simply enjoy. There is often much to be learned from the simple plaques (centre) which adorn buildings, monuments and works projects around the city. The Dominion Bridge Company, Canada's leading fabricator of steel structures, built this gateway in 1900 for two small railroad companies, which operated on the Québec side – the Pontiac Pacific and the Ottawa Gatineau Railways. When the bridge was completed, there was a big celebration. On that day in 1901, steamboats and war canoes alike crowd the Entrance Bay basin. Whistles hoot and men shout their excitement, as a photographer gets ready to capture it all on film.

MAJOR'S HILL
OVERLOOKING OPPORTUNITY

Looking like a Georgian Bay cottage scene or perhaps a sketch from the Group of Seven, this painting, by English artist Philip John Bainbrigge, provides us with a view from Barracks Hill across the lock site to what most believe to be the home of Colonel John By. By's home stood here long after he was sent home, but it was eventually destroyed by fire. In the distance stands a long gone Roman Catholic church, close to the present day site of Notre Dame Basilica. The high cliff-edge site now rings to the shouts and laughter of thousands of Ottawa's children, who come with their parents to enjoy the many family activities of the Canadian Tulip Festival. Old John By would be delighted.

Philip John Bainbrigge / NATIONAL ARCHIVES OF CANADA / C-2163

170

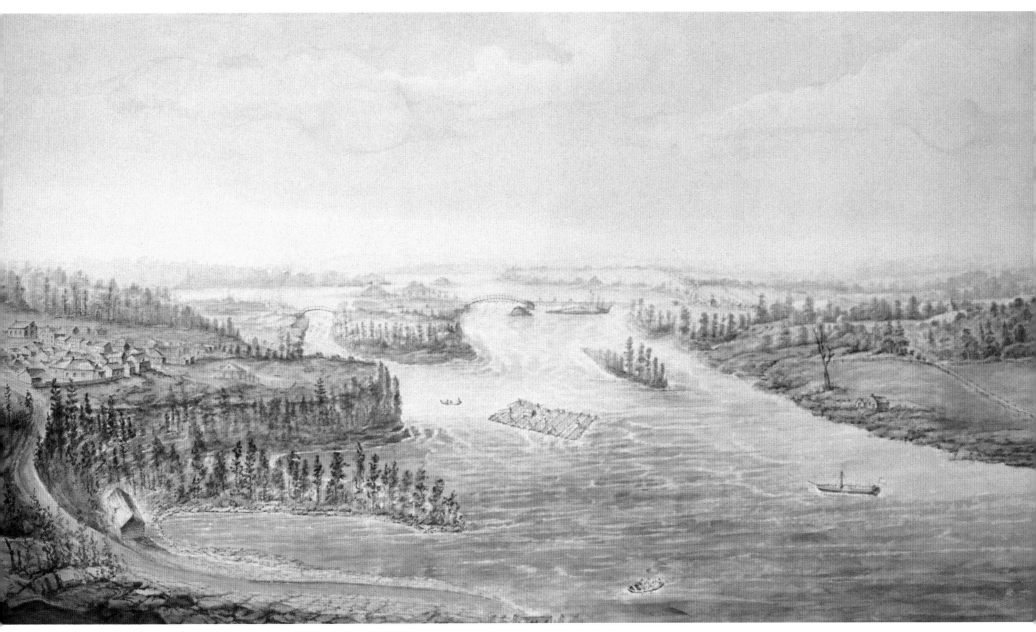

In 1830, British civil engineer John Burrows painted this view looking west over the basin and beyond to the seven spans of Union Bridge. The scene was as he saw it from the verandah of Colonel By's home on what we now call Major's Hill. Sleigh Bay in the foreground, now called Entrance Bay, was so named after an event that took place there in 1818. A Justice of the Peace, who had been brought from Perth to officiate at the wedding of Philemon Wright's son, informed him that Lower Canada (Québec) was out of his jurisdiction. The entire wedding party retired by sleigh to the Upper Canada side of the bay and the wedding was conducted while everyone stood upon the ice. Burrows, while not a particularly skilled painter, was an accomplished engineer and a key figure in the early days of Bytown. His purchase of 200 acres of land south of Barracks Hill granted him membership in the elite clique of landowners and military men who would decide the future for all of Ottawa. He eventually sold the land to Nicholas Sparks.

THE PARK THAT WAS STRIPPED OF ITS RANK

CITY OF OTTAWA ARCHIVES / CA-2936

CITY OF OTTAWA ARCHIVES / CA-2929

FIFTEEN MINUTES OF FAME SEEMS TO HAVE BEEN ALL THAT WAS ALLOTTED TO THE FATED FOUNDING FATHER OF CANADA'S CAPITAL CITY.

"A handsome cottage tastefully ornamented with rustic verandahs and trellis-work" was built for Colonel John By and his family on Colonel's Hill – named in his honour – overlooking the entrance locks to his masterpiece, the Rideau Canal. However, when By was recalled to England in 1832, his successor, Major Daniel Bolton, moved into the house and the promontory inexplicably forsook the memory of its first resident and has, ever since, carried the lesser designation, Major's Hill.

In 1866, that verdant knoll became the city's first park, the earliest project in the beautification of the National Capital. No doubt this was initiated by Lady Frances Monck who, when she arrived in Ottawa with her husband, Canada's Governor General, two years earlier, noted in her journal: "We were much disgusted with the squalid look of Ottawa." Indeed, there wasn't even a navigable road between the Governor General's residence and the parliament buildings. Viscount Monck had to be transported to Parliament along the Ottawa River in a six oar cutter manned by a Royal Navy crew.

For over one hundred years, Major's Hill Park has been a spot for Ottawans to relax and enjoy the spectacle of Parliament Hill. At the turn of the last century, children and young couples (above) enjoyed its particular delights. Though the elegant gazebos have been removed, the children and families remain. The park is also the northern anchor of a long line of tulip beds that stretch south to Dow's Lake.

Major's Hill, unlike most of Ottawa's parks, has been cherished green space since the very first days of our community. With a spectacular view up the river and of no particular industrial value, Major's Hill went from estate to civic park without any interim development. Today it is a priceless piece of Canadian history. The importance of our neighbours to the south is surely stated in the location of the new Embassy of the United States – not fifty yards from where Colonel John By directed the creation of Canada's Capital.

The shore of the Ottawa River today is as pristine as a former commercial site can be. From the north side of Nepean Point and the back of the National Gallery of Canada, we look today over stone walls and untended bushes at the back of the National War Museum (right) and the Royal Canadian Mint (centre). In the far distance, under the horizontal span of Macdonald-Cartier Bridge, we see the white frame structure of the Ottawa Rowing Club. These very same stone walls and the curving drive which they support have not changed one bit since 1924. The waterfront in this area was much more accessible in the first part of the century with boathouses, private docks, the factories of the Ketchum Boat Company and the same Ottawa Rowing Club boathouse in the distance. Along Lady Grey Drive, automobiles take in the view. The scene was one of quiet and ordered industry in 1924 and today all of it has been maintained as a park. Despite its proximity to all the tourist attractions, the spot remains virtually unknown to most Ottawans.

OTTAWA CITY, CANADA WEST.

LOWER TOWN

From Government Hill, looking down the Ottawa River and showing the locks of the Rideau Canal.

Ottawa, Published by E. Whitefield 1855

Throughout the 19th century, the expanding cities of North America were the subject of lithographed prints, which were sold to middle class citizens in lieu of the fine art which graced the halls of Ottawa's elite. In this particularly well done piece entitled "Ottawa City, Canada West", painted by Edwin Whitefield in 1855, we see the view from the former Barracks Hill. He looks across the locks to the forested knoll of Major's Hill Park and beyond to Lower Town. Gone is the home of Colonel John By, but we can clearly make out some of the new landmarks so important in the early history of Ottawa. Sappers' Bridge (upper right) spans a finished canal and a sidewheel steamer holds steady, as the water in its lock chamber is drained into the lower one. Just below it, partially hidden by the face of the hill, stands the Commissariat, home today of the Bytown Museum. In the far distance, to the left of the Notre Dame Cathedral, we can see the College of Bytown and farther left, the General Hospital started by Elizabeth Bruyère and her Grey Nuns from Montreal.

HERITAGE HOMES
WHERE HISTORY RESIDES

There are many homes in Ottawa whose heritage, judging by their size, their address or their age, is rather obvious. Then there are those whose past histories are unspoken and there for the discovery. Decades and even centuries of births, deaths, successes and failures are part of the indelible patina that shines from the old walls of many of Ottawa's homes. For many, the history is lost forever; for others it has been recorded and archived for future deed holders to find and enjoy. The country and western lyric "If these walls could talk" comes to mind when viewing these images.

CITY OF OTTAWA ARCHIVES / CA-15340

In 1904, students of Britannia's School Nº. 3 pose with their schoolmistress. Today old Nº. 3 is a fully restored upscale home in the city of Nepean and its charm and value come largely from its rich history.

CITY OF OTTAWA ARCHIVES / CA-7626

In 1882, George Stewart and his family were not of Ottawa's upper class, but they were certainly well to do. Here, they pose with their new home at 232 Cooper Street. The elegant Victorian gingerbread and the balanced lines of a fine new home were long ago erased but, for a sleuth photographer on a mission of discovery, there are clues in the brickwork that reveal it as one and the same. Though long years and careless landlords have horribly mutilated George's once-beautiful home, close inspection shows the same bay window and masonry details almost hidden by the ugly additions.

The heritage homes of Ottawa have many exquisite details that still inspire us today: porticos and verandahs, gingerbread and masonry, arches and gables, quoins and fascias. The precise balance between fenestration and

roofline, between vertical and horizontal, is seemingly unattainable for many of Ottawa's present day architects. In the last century, the city must have been inundated with a plethora of excellent and careful residential

designers, judging by the proliferation and quality of their creations. They find no worthy match in the token styles of today's suburban sprawl.

BYWARD MARKET
FRESH, FREINDLY, FAMILIAR

The Byward Market has, since the beginning of Ottawa's history, been the heart, soul, purse and breadbasket of a thriving community. In Paul Alfred's richly textured painting from 1928, we see that the delicious atmosphere of farm produce and chaotic traffic has been the hallmark of the Market for all time. The turreted mansard roof of the old Market Building on Byward Street is seen from York Street looking east. Lapointe's Fish Market, a long-standing Ottawa establishment, was obviously located here in the 1920s. The yellow brick building, seen here at the southeast corner of William and York, now caters to tourists as a seafood restaurant.

Paul Alfred / NATIONAL ARCHIVES OF CANADA / C-010536

Winter or summer, the market has always been a beehive of activity. In the cold winter light, captured by Franklin Brownell in the early 1900s, merchants and shoppers crowd the streets. Judging by the light, this is a view north to the often reconstituted main Market Building between Byward and William Streets. The air is crisp, with the snow squeaking underfoot. One can almost hear the snort and stomp of the draught horses, the jingle of sleigh bells and the shouts and laughter of a people who, like we today, enjoyed an outing to the marvellous Market.

Looking southwest from 500 feet above Byward, we can see clearly the conditions that were about to make or break the Market. Union Station and its unsightly tracks combine with Postal Station "A" and its vast parking lot to effectively cut off the area from Upper Town. Other long gone buildings, like the National Defence temporary buildings and the Roxborough Apartments in front of the Lord Elgin, can be seen. The market is largely isolated and left to develop on its own, but it deteriorates instead. Urban renewal is focused on Upper Town and the buildings of the Byward Market begin to show their age. They are not properly maintained and the place develops a decrepit air of poverty and unruliness. By the late 1960s, the always active Market is somewhat of a joke among suburbanites, who are more likely to frequent the new malls and supermarkets. A multitude of rough drinking establishments and a problem with prostitution does not help to put Byward back on its feet.

Being left to wither on the vine, while Upper Town gets its cold-hearted facelift, proves a blessing in disguise. The age of heritage groups and enlightened planners is dawning. Classic and heritage buildings, which only a few years ago would be considered a blight, are seen for what they are – human scale buildings of wonderful detail which resonate with the innate personality of the Ottawa landscape. Most are quickly deemed of historic importance and are indexed for salvation. From the middle 1970s to the present day, the Market undergoes a long process of remarkable rejuvenation. In this aerial over the Byward Market in 1960, we see that it has remained completely intact and free of the beastly glass towers of Upper Town. Today, much of what we see remains and much of what was lost is being recaptured in upscale infill projects, which combine residential and retail uses.

Today, the Byward Market from the air looks much as it did in 1960. The streets are crowded with vegetable and flower stalls and parked cars. But at street level, the change is astonishing. The Market is a fashionable Epicurean enclave of fabulous restaurants of every kind. Its lucrative bars and nightclubs draw enormous crowds all year round and when the sun sets, the action begins. Cruising cars, strolling tourists and Ottawa's hip young professionals school around the Market Building and adjoining streets. A warm summer night at one of the outdoor terraces on Clarence Street is a wonderful urban experience rivaling any city on the planet. Late into the early morning hours, Upper Town lawyers rub shoulders with hobos, bikers with students, squeegee kids with tourists.

Between the restaurants stand a mixture of wonderful boutiques and curio shops, cluttered workwear stores of rich character and delicatessens thick with the smells of sausage and herbs. The Market is now a mecca for Ottawa's design elite, with many graphic design, architectural, multi-media and advertising companies surrounding themselves with the creative excitement. Clients jump at the chance to meet their consultants for lunch in one of the many fine establishments. A quick tour of the vegetable stalls before heading home nets local business people fresh produce for tonight's dinner. The immense Rideau Centre shopping complex, the Westin Hotel and Congress Center (top photo) repeat the scale of their industrial predecessors, but now these new hotels and facilities and those to the east work to bring tourists and shoppers to the Market. What goes around, comes around. Upper Town's 1960s and '70s development caused the near demise of the Byward Market, but now the tables have turned. The glass canyons of Upper Town are like a ghost town on weekends or when the sun goes down. The Market today is more alive than it has ever been and Ottawa is a better city for it.

The 20th century has produced more substantial change to the human condition than any other, but at the close of the millennium, it's the old values that have resurfaced and remain strong. In these four images, we see an urban meeting place stand virtually unchanged for almost a century, while the swirl of technology eddies around it. The essential elements, which attracted Ottawans as far back as Colonel By's time, remain – shared experience, excitement, ownership, culture and production.

In 1910 (top left), though the first car has already made its debut, the horse is king. Looking across George Street, we peer not only down Byward Street, but also down the corridor of history. Horse drawn farmer's carts have made the early morning journey into town from outlying farms. Carriages belonging to shoppers take home the produce or circle the chaos looking for a good place to park.

In only 10 years (middle left), the technology change is spectacular. The horse has been deposed and the shiny new vehicles of the region's farmers give meaning to the new phrase – "truck farmers". While the odd horse drawn carriage is not a thing to be gawked at in the early 1920s, it is, regardless, a thing of the past. Despite the coming of the automobile, the stalls, buildings, awnings and traffic have remained untouched.

In 1950 (bottom left), the cars are bigger and more streamlined, but business goes on as usual. The exciting growth of the city parallels that of the country, which has hit its stride following WWII. The main market building has been replaced by a new and improved structure, offering covered yet open areas for the sale of produce.

Today, Byward Market is an active and successful outdoor grocery store. In-season produce from around the Ottawa River Valley fills the stalls and people come from all over the city for the freshness, the price and the atmosphere.

When the streets of Bytown were first laid out, both York and George Street were easily twice as wide as standard streets in the plan. One might speculate that this was designed specifically to meet the needs of a market, where local farmers and hunters could sell their wares. Since those early days, York Street has been one of Ottawa's busiest streets. In 1911, the street was like the old west. Dirt covered roadways and horse drawn vehicles must certainly have made for some high smells on a hot summer day. Many of the same buildings can be seen in both of the photographs above.

Though the city had plenty of green grocers and butchers back in 1921, there was only one supermarket where city folk could do some one-stop shopping – the Byward Market. The corner of Byward and York Streets was, as it is today, a traffic nightmare. Aimless shoppers, lurching carriages, bicycles, cars and crowded stalls made the going slow, even back then.

Today, the farmers' market has been reduced in size, since many of the farm products and the ways in which they were sold are no longer fashionable. Right up to the 1950s, shoppers could have a chicken, rabbit or goose slaughtered right in front of them. Animals for food were once part of the scene on York Street, but sensibilities being what they are, people nowadays prefer their meat pre-dressed at a butcher shop. Today the large open space is dedicated to cars and restaurant terraces. Desperate shoppers looking for the perfect spot still circle this block several times before they find one.

It's early morning at the corner of Byward and York Streets. The day's crowd of shoppers has yet to come. In the distance the Peace Tower rings out eight o'clock as it has done for almost every day since 1927. The street will soon be alive with office workers, shoppers and tourists and another day in the busy life of the Byward Market will be underway.

HORSE SENSE

SHARING A HOME WITH HORSES IS A BIZARRE WAY TO GET AROUND THE LAW, BUT THIS IS EXACTLY HOW ONE RESOURCEFUL LIVERYMAN IS SAID TO HAVE COPED WITH A BAN PLACED BY CITY COUNCIL ON THE ERECTION OF STABLES IN OTTAWA IN THE LATE 1920S.

The horse lover accommodated both the law and his stock by stabling his animals in his basement. And it worked. For a while. Then the neighbourhood objected and political pressure ensued, resulting eventually in the passing of yet another by-law, this time prohibiting the keeping of almost all livestock within the city limits.

The only stable to survive the by-law has been operated for a hundred years by the horse-trading Cundell ("It's in the blood") Family. A peaceful oasis of life at animal-speed in the thick of urban noise and commotion, the stable delights those who stumble across its unobtrusive presence on York Street in the bustling Byward Market area.

Johnny Cundell, third generation operator, took to the business naturally. For him, horses have always been "part of the family" and he remembers vividly a sense of loss as a child when a favourite was traded. His father, Fred, first handed him the reins – literally – when he was a youngster, just as his father, William, had done for him. In those days, city streets offered little threat to a team of working horses and their driver – indeed, Cundell teams helped excavate the foundations of the growing city and kept its winter streets free of obstructive snow. Today, the operation largely serves the pleasure industry, participating in weddings, parades and special events and offering wagon and sleigh rides. And Johnny is confident that at least one of his five children will continue the tradition into its second century.

Cundell horses are so city-smart they know enough to stop at red lights – "Though they're not so good on stop signs," sighs Johnny – and to move on when the lights turn green. That may just make them smarter than the urban sophisticates who yelled "Fire!" when, one frigid winter day, they spotted some fresh horse "nuggets" steaming in the stable yard.

The Cundell family horses have always been working animals. Though they now give easy-going wagon and carriage rides, they were once hard pulling draught horses. Here (opposite main), the Cundell crew poses with their team during the construction of the Ottawa Airport between the wars. If you want to take a ride on the world's slowest time machine, hop on the Cundell wagon. For decades, their horses have delighted children and lovers with the wonders of horse drawn locomotion. In the 1950s (opposite left), the children of Rockcliffe got a kick out of the communal warmth of a winter ride, just as they still do in 1999 (opposite right). The romance of a carriage ride through New Edinburgh and Rockcliffe (opposite centre) inspires newly weds on that most important day.

The Cundell stable on York Street still turns heads, when a strong horse suddenly appears from between two houses. Children are particularly attracted to John Cundell's work, petting and riding the horses or catching the wagon for a few circuits of the Byward Market, while Mom and Dad do a little Christmas shopping.

The Market and its surrounding shops and monuments are rich in the details that make life in Ottawa so wonderful. History and architecture combine with fine food and the

camaraderie of a pub; seasonal produce and spirituality with sunlight and art; or the community with the nation. The experience is one for all senses: the smell of fresh-brewed coffee,

the spirited sounds of the buskers, the riotous colours of flowers and vegetables, the taste of honey and maple syrup and the texture of stone and bronze.

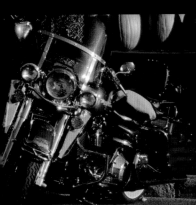

While the Byward Market was, and is still, not the only open-air market in Ottawa, it is the biggest and longest-standing. The centre of the Byward Market has always been the block bounded by William on the east and Byward on the west. On this block, have existed a number of versions of the main market building. Today's building (above), dates from several decades ago, but has been recently redesigned and refurbished. In the summer, it is surrounded by stalls selling everything from tomatoes to South American hammocks and from silver jewelry to Beavertails, Ottawa's official pastry. The stalls and outlets are choked with shoppers, and traffic, though slow and chaotic, is never of the stressful variety. People come here for one reason – the shopping is made enjoyable because each purchase is a happy social experience.

On a winter night, the strolling crowds are gone, but the Market sparkles with the enticing light of shop interiors. When the Christmas season is close at hand, and the days are not too bitter, the crowds will return to the stalls for handmade wreaths, Christmas trees, firewood and gifts. The warmth of coffee shops beckons and pubs are especially busy.

CITY OF OTTAWA ARCHIVES / CA-1806

NATIONAL ARCHIVES OF CANADA / C-5633

In this 1922 photograph, we see an almost identical scene to that portrayed in Paul Alfred's wonderful painting on page 160. Lapointe's fish market was located at this northern end of the central structure during the 1920s.

The central market building has had several forms, such as this stone structure, pictured in 1900. The vernacular of the market building has always included sweeping rooflines and shed-roofed stalls, around which the commercial activity has swarmed. The same building can be seen in Franklin Brownell's painting on page 161.

Lapointe's Fish Market is a Byward Market and Ottawa institution. For as long as Canada has been a country, the fishmongers of this small business have offered a net full of the best seafood available anywhere. In 1880, Lapointe's well turned out staff of seafood experts pose proudly in front of their store. A sign hangs at right, proclaiming their pedigree – "By Appointment to His Excellency the Governor General"

Today, the best salmon, mussels, oysters and lobsters can still be found right at the heart of the Byward Market and 1,000 kilometers from the nearest ocean. The Lapointe legacy of excellence lives on with its knowledgeable staff, posing outside their store on Byward Street.

For decades, the Irving Rivers outerwear and dry goods store at the corner of Byward and York has been the source of low cost goods such as clothing, camping equipment, boots and assorted paraphernalia. The Rivers' store slogan "We Corner the Market" would not apply to his ancestor's original fruit and vegetable shop in the 1920's, which was not at the corner, but in the middle of the block north. The original location of the Rivers' store on Byward is a now a diner in the tradition of the finest roadhouses of North America. Some of Ottawa's most creative individuals have been known to frequent its booths for breakfast and families line up to get a table in the evenings and on weekends.

At the corner of Murray and Sussex, there once stood the tobacco shop of J.C. Ferland who obviously believed that "Everyone Smokes Chum Tobacco". The building where old Mr. Ferland used to sell his pipes, cigars, cigarettes and tobacco is now a snug and friendly pub called the Earl of Sussex. In the summer, the "Earl's" terrace is alive with people who like their sun warm, their beer cold and their service friendly.

The Cleroux family name is synonymous with the Byward Market. For over a century the ever-expanding family of Cleroux farmers has occupied more than a few market stalls, both in the Byward and Parkdale open air markets. Madame Laurence Cleroux, whose father opened his stall at the turn of the century, still works the market at the corner of Byward and George in all types of weather. In winter months when the farm produce would freeze if you could get it, she sells handmade Christmas wreaths and boughs.

Snugged up tight to weather the next winter storm, the market building looks desolate in this early Sunday morning shot. But the Market is no stranger to storms. On Monday, September 17, 1846, there arose the most famous of all Ottawa storms and it was not one of snow or wind. A meeting had been called to prepare a non-partisan welcome for Governor General Lord Elgin on his tour of the region, with the hopes of his consideration of Bytown as the site of the new capital. Instead of bringing townsfolk together, it had the opposite effect of polarizing the community. The city was facing a post-canal construction depression and tempers were already at the boiling point. A scuffle turned into a punch-up, which got out of control when a riot broke out. Many were hurt and one killed. Because the stone was the weapon of choice for the fracas, the fight went down in history as the Stony Monday Riot.

NATIONAL ARCHIVES OF CANADA / PA-85978

The corner is much the same as it was at the turn of the century. The small stone building at the extreme left is a popular bar called "Stoney's", named after the divisive riot that raged outside its front door in 1849.

The scene at the southeast corner of William and York streets in the 1920s was not too different from what one would see on a winter's day today. Wood sellers stand hunched against the cold and the future location of Stoney's bar (centre) is then the Richelieu Hotel, which sheltered citizens during the Stony Monday riot.

If the sun won't shine on a cold winter's day, at least the coming of the night will bring the bright and warm invitation of shop windows to deflect the cold from one's heart.

A double decker bus, with an open upper deck, gives riders the second best vantagepoint from which to experience the colour, smells and sounds of the Byward Market. The best, of course, would be to get out on foot and interact with the sellers under their colourful awnings; to squeeze the tomatoes, smell the flowers and taste the samples of fresh fruit and vegetables that are always offered.

MILE OF HISTORY

OTTAWA AS WE ONCE WERE

Not many buildings, of such unassuming style as 541 Sussex Drive (above), can claim such rich history and importance to the city of Ottawa and to Canada. Originally, it had been constructed as the British Hotel, then enlarged and used as a barracks and then was returned to hotel use as the Clarendon Hotel. In 1880, it was acquired by the government to house the Geological Survey, an important research activity of the new Canada. Also incorporated in the facility was the new National Gallery, which housed works by the Canadian Academy of Arts. This facility, administered by the Academy, would become the nucleus of the great, and future, world-class National Gallery of Canada. Various federal departments and agencies have occupied this site since those days and today it is managed by the National Capital Commission. It presently houses restaurants and coffee shops, as well as design professionals and the Embassy of the Czech Republic.

In 1910, much of Ottawa's growth and activity was recorded for posterity by photographers. This view shows the Geological Survey Building and the second block of what we now call the "Mile of History". Government planners, wishing to preserve Ottawa's history for all of Canada, coined the phrase and endeavoured to refurbish the length of Sussex Drive. It was already too late for the long line of elegant structures (right) on the west side of the street, which backed onto a twenty-foot escarpment. These were demolished to make way for the Connaught Building, as well as the wartime temporary buildings that occupied the present site of the new Embassy of the United States.

CITY OF OTTAWA ARCHIVES

At lower left, the citizens of Ottawa flock to the newly established Canadian Academy of Arts for the opening of its first major exhibition in the 1880s. The exhibition was first called for by Governor General, the Marquess of Lorne, a champion of the arts for the new country. Before the National Gallery was housed in its present facility, it occupied an office building on Elgin Street, which became known as the Lorne Building. The Sussex Drive portion (the former British Hotel) of the Geographic Survey Building, was later altered (above left) from a four-storey building to its present three-storey configuration. The Mile of History (above) features many private galleries as well, catering primarily to Ottawans and tourists.

One of the earliest structures on Sussex Street still in existence, Notre Dame Basilica stands facing prominently up river. French Catholic raftsmen, back in 1848, who were about to risk their lives on the Chaudière slides, could easily see its twin 170-foot steeples and make a silent prayer to the Virgin. In fact, the golden statue of the Blessed Virgin and Child, which stands between the spires, was purchased by the lumbermen. Originally called a Cathedral, it has since been upgraded to Basilica status.

It was from the rectory of this large church, in 1849, that the first Catholic Bishop of Bytown, Bishop Joseph-Eugène Bruno Guigues (namesake of Guigues Street), directed the building of a new education facility right next door on Sussex. The Collège de Bytown (far left) was a college and seminary with teaching priests and brothers from the order known as the Oblates of Mary Immaculate. Soon the school had moved to new a location in Sandy Hill, acquired a higher status, and had become known as the University of Ottawa. The Oblate hold on the administration of the university was to last well into the 1970s and its bilingual nature today is a direct result of the vision of Guigues. The building was subsequently operated as the Hôtel de Champagne and was turned over in 1870 to be used as an elementary school. This facility was the Christian Brothers School and was part of the Ottawa Separate School Board. Today, it houses several government offices.

The National Gallery of Canada, located on the great open plaza at the corner of St. Patrick Street and Sussex Drive is, like the Museum of Civilization, one of the jewels in the crown of Canada's Capital. The crystal-like facets of the Moshe Safdie design reflect visual qualities to be found in the Parliament Buildings and in particular the Parliamentary Library. The Gallery houses an incredible permanent collection, featuring many diverse works, including those by Canada's Group of Seven. Several impressive touring exhibitions have also passed through its grand galleries in recent years, including Van Gogh, Degas, Renoir and Picasso.

In summer months the plaza comes alive with tourists and music lovers, who come to enjoy the open-air concerts and each other's company in the Gallery's amphitheatre.

The "Mile of History" passes in grand fashion past the National Gallery plaza. A long line of curio, book, fashion and antique shops takes advantage of both the sunlight and the crowds drawn to the attractions of the area.

THE IMPROBABILITY OF CHOICE THINKING

THE MOST IMPROBABLE OF CIRCUMSTANCES SPAWNED THE CITY'S FIRST SEAT OF HIGHER LEARNING, THE UNIVERSITY OF OTTAWA.

In 1848, Bytown still struggled under its reputation for lawlessness. Not yet officially incorporated as a town, much less a city, the fledgling community was also suffering through a depression so severe it had lost one-quarter of its population of some 7,000 souls, due to a cyclical collapse of the essential lumber trade and to the crash of the 15-year old Rideau Canal as a transportation route, usurped by the newly completed canals of the St. Lawrence River system.

It was in the midst of such instability and distress some 150 years ago that Bishop Bruno Guigues was inspired to found an institution of erudite learning – not trades or simple literacy, but the classics: Greek, Latin and religion. In both English and French. The boldness of his action and the immediate receptivity of the struggling community which right away enrolled some 60 of its youth in this college of higher knowledge vividly reveals the spirit of contagious optimism coupled with an abiding passion for ongoing transformation upon which the city was founded.

It is small wonder, then, that Canada's national newspaper, The Globe and Mail, when choosing the National Capital as a most desirable destination for business at the approach to the 21st century, stated that Ottawa provides an environment in which the "creativity" of "choice thinkers" most successfully "flourishes."

Monseigneur Bruno Guigues, Bishop of the Diocese of Bytown, created the first school of higher education in the city, and he did it with money from his own pocket. His statue now stands near the grounds of the old College of Bytown, where it looks out across the plaza towards Parliament, the National Gallery of Canada and the Ottawa River Valley. When our forefathers made their contributions to our present state, they most likely did so without full knowledge that what they were doing would reverberate down through the centuries. It may be just a guess, but one can bet that Bruno Guigues fully understood what he was setting in motion.

The bilingual St. Joseph's College of Bytown was the birthplace of Ottawa's university tradition. The first Principal of the school was Père Henri Tabaret of the Oblates of Mary Immaculate. His name lives on at Tabaret Hall, one of the oldest buildings on the huge urban campus. Today, thousands of students from all over Canada and the world receive undergraduate and post-graduate education in both of Ottawa's founding languages.

In 1893, this was the scene from Sandy Hill, a fashionable residential district to the east of the city's growing core. Between Sandy Hill and the canal lies an area of lower income housing, hotels and offices, which is today the site of the Rideau Centre and the Congress Centre.

Standing on top of a building (perhaps Ottawa University) in Sandy Hill in 1903, a photographer takes in the new developments in Ottawa's central core. The railroad can now be seen reaching to the future site of Union Station. The large building, with the square tower across the canal (left background) is the old City Hall at the corner of Queen and Elgin Streets. It was abandoned in 1931 after it was destroyed by fire.

Standing atop a high building at Ottawa University today, another recorder of Ottawa's history captures the scene nearly a century later. In the centre stands the Headquarters of the Department of National Defence, which sits along the canal. In the foreground, the multiple buildings of the University of Ottawa give testament to Bishop Bruno Guigues' goal to offer higher education to young Bytowners.

In 1844, the Albion Hotel was constructed on what was then called Court House Avenue, at the corner of Nicholas Street. Strategically placed near the new Court House, it thrived throughout the years. The original hotel was the structure facing Nicholas. In this photo taken in 1875, we can see the large addition that was added to the east, along what was to become Daly Avenue. Either photographers had a way of attracting attention in those days, or there was some eventful reason why so many citizens have turned out to grace the hotel's balconies and sidewalks.

Today, the old Albion Hotel has been demolished, making way for a larger Novotel Hotel complex. The second wing of the old hotel appears to still be here, but it too was knocked down and a new building of the same dimensions and style was erected on the same site.

Until 1842, the nearest court and jail were in the town of Perth, Ontario, 60 miles to the west. Ottawa's new Court House, which was built that year, included a jail in the basement. However, the barred windows opened right at street level, allowing friends to pass liquor and even breakout tools to jailed scofflaws. The present purpose-built jailhouse came into existence in 1862. The last public hanging in Canada was held here on February 11, 1869. The convicted assassin of Thomas D'Arcy McGee, a Fenian sympathizer by the name of Patrick James Whelan, swung from the gallows on the east side of the building.

Today, the jailhouse functions as one of the world's most interesting youth hostels. Students and budget-minded travellers can spend the night in the slammer. The hospitality has improved since the turn of the century, but it is said that the ghost of Whelan still walks the halls at night. The gallows still exists and can be viewed from Waller Street.

AN EXCEPTIONAL ECCENTRIC

From Sussex Drive, we are looking east along the fast-developing Rideau Street facade in 1898. We see the area where Charles Ogilvy was building his business on good value and fine service. An electric streetcar clatters up the incline to the corner of Sussex, past a row of buildings, which are now the site of the Rideau Centre.

In 1925, the Charles Ogilvy store had grown to encompass an entire city block. There isn't an Ottawan alive, who grew up here in the '50s and '60s, who doesn't remember the beautiful white gloved and kilted elevator attendants, who so graciously and silently took them up to men's wear...ladies' wear... housewares...

Charles Ogilvy and his wife relax outside their house on Buena Vista Road, in the Village of Rockcliffe Park.

IDEALISTIC TRAILBLAZERS ARE NEXT TO COMMONPLACE THROUGHOUT OTTAWA'S HISTORY. CHARLES OGILVY WAS ONE SUCH VISIONARY.

In November 1887, he opened a small dry goods store at 92 Rideau Street and carefully tended his business until it expanded to cover most of a city block. The secret of his success lay in not only meeting the needs of his customers but also those of his many employees. In the 1930s, Ogilvy took the unusual step of establishing a pension plan for his staff. He then went on to top this generosity before his death in 1950 by actually giving the store to the employees, whom he regarded as his family.

The magnanimous Scotsman's only self-indulgence – one might even say eccentricity – was to have three homes built in various areas of town, each one identical to the other two, providing him the comfort of familiar surroundings no matter where he travelled in the city.

Looking west on Rideau Street in 1898, we are able to orient ourselves fairly quickly with the East Block of the Parliament Buildings in the background. We are looking at the north side of the block, east of Sussex Drive. A couple of curs chase a man and his carriage along Rideau Street. Judging by the position of horses in this photo and in many others previous, it did not matter which side of the street one drove on. Today, the streetscape has many similar qualities, but the commerce on the street has lost some of its panache, set back many years by the failed Rideau Street Bus Mall. The well-intentioned, enclosed sidewalk along Rideau Street, was built at the same time as the Rideau Centre, but quickly turned into a panhandling nightmare for retailers. By the time the mistake was rectified and the hideous enclosures removed, it was too late. The end had come for many retailers including Ogilvy's.

Moving further east on Rideau Street in 1898, we turn and face west again. This time we can see buildings at the turn of the century that remain in existence today. The building at right in the old photo is today the home of a Moore's men's store. Looking further up the street, the building on the corner of the next block still lives on. The construction of the Rideau Centre and the enlarging of the Bay store wiped out two well-known but short streets in this area - Freiman Street and Mosgrove Street. Freiman Street ran alongside A.J. Freiman's quintessential Ottawa department store, which was still running strong until bought up by the Hudson's Bay Company in the 1970s. Today' the interior street that runs through the ground floor of the Bay is actually Freiman Street.

Do Not Go Gently Into That Good Night

OTTAWA WOULD STILL BE IN THE DARK AGES, LITERALLY, HAD SOME EARLY MEMBERS OF THE COMMUNITY HAD THEIR WAY.

Outside illumination began with a whale oil lamp over each of the town's two public wells. Then, in the 1850s, gas lamps were introduced on Rideau and Sussex streets. However, by decree of City Council, these lamps were to be lit only during the dark phases of the moon, regardless of how black the night due to cloud or weather conditions.

In 1882, two electric arc lamps were installed outside Levi Young's mill on Lebreton Flats, drawing hundreds of people every evening to marvel at the sight. Detractors, meanwhile, uttered dire warnings about the consequences of "turning night into day."

It was only with a good deal of reservation that City Council began installing arc lights on city streets some four years later. "Daylight has been such a cheap blessing hitherto that the payment of $150,000 per annum for a little more of it will scarcely meet with the approbation of those who take a practical view of the subject," warned Mayor Charles Mackintosh.

Between 1885 and 1890, incandescent lighting was introduced into homes, up to ten bulbs on one circuit so that when one bulb was turned on or off, all the bulbs would follow suit. As can be imagined, trouble would erupt when a homeowner who shared a circuit with a neighbour persisted in flicking the lights to demonstrate to visitors the "miracle" of electricity.

In 1902, there was no better place for some of the first electric street lamps in the city than on the central promenade of the Parliament Buildings. Today, the Parliament Buildings are lit at night with spectacular flood lamps in the summer months and eye-popping Christmas lights in the winter.

CITY OF OTTAWA ARCHIVES / CA-1508

By 1877, gas lamps were part of the streetscape in Ottawa. At the railing around the open area between Sappers' Bridge and Dufferin Bridge, gas lanterns are used to illuminate the sidewalk for wary pedestrians.

NATIONAL ARCHIVES OF CANADA / PA-24945

ONCE THEY GRASPED THE CONCEPT...

THE WORLD'S FIRST LONG-DISTANCE RADIO BROADCAST — RECEIVED FROM MORE THAN 150 KILOMETRES (100 MILES) AWAY — THRILLED A CROWD OF 500 GATHERED AT THE CHATEAU LAURIER HOTEL ON MAY 20TH, 1920. THIS WAS A FAR CRY INDEED FROM THE DAYS IN 1850 WHEN LOCAL FARMERS REGULARLY PLUNGED OTTAWA INTO ISOLATION FROM THE REST OF THE WORLD BY CUTTING SECTIONS OF THE NEWLY INSTALLED TELEGRAPH LINES THAT LINKED THE CITY TO MONTREAL. THEY THEN USED THE WIRE TO BIND THEIR LOADS OF PRODUCE AS THEY HEADED INTO TOWN TO MARKET.

A quarter of a century later, on September 21st, 1877, the city's first telephone line was strung between the Prime Minister's Office and the residence of the Governor General, Lord Dufferin. However, the Prime Minister would have had the newfangled contraption disconnected had it not been for the insistence of Lady Dufferin, who liked to entertain her Rideau Hall guests by accompanying Capt. François de B. Gourdeau of the Marine Department on the piano as he sang over the telephone from the Prime Minister's Office.

A century later, Ottawa is recognized throughout the world as a trailblazer in telecommunications.

The cities of Nepean and Kanata have made the National Capital region the Silicon Valley of the North. Over seven hundred high-technology companies making both software and hardware, are located throughout many high-tech parks, campuses and downtown office buildings. The brightest star in the region's technology galaxy is Nortel Networks, a.k.a. Northern Telecom, one of the largest of its kind on the planet. Nortel conceives, designs, tests and builds advanced telecommunications equipment and software for clients around the world. They operate out of several large buildings around Kanata and Nepean, but their main Carling Avenue Campus (above) is more than just visually the "temple of telecommunications".

The architects of the Capital's high-technology renaissance, are Michael Cowpland and Terry Matthews, the founders of the Mitel Corporation. Today, Cowpland's Corel Corporation (lower right) and Matthews' Newbridge Networks Corporation (lower left) are world leaders and employers of thousands of the region's citizens.

Spar Aerospace, the designers and the builders of the Space Shuttle's remote manipulator arm and the poster child of high technology in Canada in the 1980s, have recently undergone many corporate changes. Here, Spar technicians undertake test and evaluation tasks on another world-beating project.

AUTUMN
A HARVEST OF COLOUR

With the coming of fall, Ottawans are of two minds. We lament the passing of yet another warm and languid summer and start to feel the exhilaration that the increasingly colder mornings bring. Soon it will be winter, time for skating on the canal, skiing in the Gatineaus or tobogganing at the Central Experimental Farm. Getting out to enjoy the breathtaking colour of the fall leaves throughout the region is the perfect way to make the transition.

Miss SBJ sweeps quietly up the canal on a fall afternoon. The back deck is a great spot to catch the last warm rays of the season and to watch the passing parade of fall colour.

The Prime Minister of Canada can take off a few hours from his or her busy schedule during the fall sitting of Parliament and enjoy the leaves from the official Prime Ministerial summer residence on private Harrington Lake.

Flying over the main quadrangle in front of Ottawa University's Tabaret Hall, we see that the fall colours have offered students yet another distraction.

Cyclists and runners alike can enjoy autumn and exercise at the same time. A favourite route for both is up Colonel By Drive to Union Station, back down Queen Elizabeth Drive, around Dow's Lake to the Arboretum at the Central Experimental Farm, across Hartwell's Locks at Carleton University and then all the way back up town again. This route provides nearly twenty kilometres of superb and easy cycling or running and the best of the city's parks in their fall splendour. The pathways around the canal are smoothly paved and run in and out of the trees while remaining close to the canal all the way.

During late spring and early summer, the Musical Ride offers up evening demonstrations of their spectacular precision horsemanship to the citizens of Ottawa. And the citizens of Ottawa love a free show. The setting sun warms the buildings and grounds of the RCMP 'N' Division and Musical Ride stables near the eastern end of Rockcliffe Park. In the sky, a giant hot air balloon, commemorating the 125th Anniversary of the founding of the Northwest Mounted Police in 1874, drifts silently eastward on the evening breeze. Below, in the Musical Ride amphitheatre, the Commissioner of the RCMP stands ready to take the salute from the "Ride" during their romantic Sunset Ceremony. At right, two members of "The Force", celebrating the 25th anniversary of women in the ranks, lower the flag at the setting of the sun.

The rich green foliage and warm hues of a sun setting over the western stretches of the Ottawa River are the hallmarks of summertime in Ottawa. Throughout this book, we have seen many black and white photographs chronicling the unique history of Canada's Capital. Although rich in detail, these photographs have a way of portraying Ottawa as a grey and sometimes lifeless town. But rest assured that Bytown and Ottawa were always colourful. The skies were just as blue in Colonel By's time, the trees just as green in MacKenzie King's and the people were never grey. They were, as they are today, busy, determined, curious and in love with their city. They loved to work. They loved to relax. They loved to be together.

We wander Ottawa like it is our house, the streets like our corridors, the buildings like our rooms. But we were born to it. Our ancestors built it from the very earth on which it stands and left it for us. Each generation made their mark, added their bit and affected the destiny of this once tiny community on the river. Ottawa is a work in progress and it is our duty to continue; to have vision as Thomas MacKay and Colonel By had; to work hard like Braddish Billings and Philemon Wright did; and to give something back to our city like Bruno Guigues and to our country as did MacKenzie King. And if, when the sun sets, we can leave Ottawa a better place than we found it, we will have found our place in history.

DAVE O'MALLEY *came to Ottawa in 1954 with his parents Hugh and Kitty and their children. Though born a Nova Scotian, he is an Ottawan at heart. Dave has a degree in Architecture from Carleton University and is president of a graphic design company located at the heart of the Byward Market. He has been a strong supporter of the community through his involvement in such events as the National Capital Air Show, Canadian Tulip Festival, Museums Day, and the Ottawa Bluesfest.*

His proudest accomplishment is his part in the raising of two extraordinary daughters, Lauren and Merrill. He has shared with and nurtured in them a love for this wonderful city. There is no amount of money or promise that could entice Dave to take up his roots and move.

ROSALIND TOSH *wasn't supposed to be a writer, but then neither was she supposed to be a Sagittarian, a Canadian nor an historian. However, the sign of the archer claimed her, ready or not, some five decades ago in Ireland and then, unkindly thwarted in love twenty-four years later, she herself claimed Canada as a place of refuge, now her chosen home. The seductive power of historic research is a very recent and unexpected experience for her, first undertaken as a favour for a friend and then captivating her as it breathed soul and life into the nooks and crannies and the bricks and mortar of her favourite city, Ottawa.*

It was another friend's temporary misfortune twenty years ago that thrust her by chance from the peripherals of high technology into the role of a writer. His sickbed plea for someone to replace him as editor of an Ottawa community newspaper just couldn't be denied and, to her joy and amazement, she discovered that her voice flowed most fluently through the pen. She has been writing ever since.

JACQUELIN HOLZMAN *believes there is no view of her home town more evocative than the one forming the backdrop to this photo, showcasing as it does the magnificent river which carried explorers into the heart of Canada, the masterpiece of a canal which brought Ottawa's founding father Colonel John By, and the majestic seat of government which makes the city a symbolic home for all Canadians.*

First as a volunteer and then as a professional, Jackie has devoted forty-five years of her life to enabling residents of this beautiful city to achieve their own goals. Before taking her seat on Ottawa City Council for fifteen years, she was a planner of rehabilitation, housing, transportation and employment programs for the elderly and persons with special needs. She served as Ottawa's Mayor from 1991 until her retirement in 1997.

In 1998, Jackie was appointed chairman of the Ottawa Congress Centre, was awarded an Honorary Doctorate from the University of Ottawa for her community service, and became an articulate public advocate for the early diagnosis of breast cancer following her own personal surgery. She is married to John Rutherford and is the mother of four and grandmother of four.

JOHN McQUARRIE *is an Ottawa photographer whose major commercial clients include Coors, Marlboro, McDonnell Douglas and Lockheed. But his real passion is producing coffee table books. Previous titles include:*
 Canadian Wings
 Canadian Fighter Pilot
 'Til We Meet Again
 Between The Lines
 Cowboyin'
 Rodeoin'
 The Great Centennial Cattle Drive
 Montana Cowboyin'
 New Mexico Cowboyin'

The earlier works focused on the Canadian Air Force from World War II to the Gulf War, and the Canadian Armed Forces in their role as Peacekeepers. John then turned his lens on the cattle business and working cowboys.

Future books will include a series of "Then & Now" projects with Above Canada, Then & Now scheduled for release in the Fall of 1999. Similar titles on Vancouver and Toronto will follow. He also intends to produce a photographic portrait of Scotland's single malt whisky industry.

BIBLIOGRAPHY

Gatineau Park, An Intimate Portrait, J. David Andrews, Dynamic Light

Ottawa An Illustrated History, John H. Taylor, James Lorimer & Company (Toronto), 1986

Ottawa, City of the Big Ears, Robert Haig, Haig and Haig Publishing Co. (Ottawa), 1969

Ottawa Old & New, Lucien Brault, Ottawa Historical Information Institute (Ottawa), 1946

Ottawa The Capital of Canada, Shirley E. Woods Jr., Doubleday (Toronto & New York), 1980

Report on Business Magazine, The Globe and Mail (Toronto), August 1994 & 1995

The Genesis of Our Capital, Hamnett P. Hill, Historical Society of Ottawa (Ottawa), 1935

The Hub and the Spokes or the Capital and Its Environs, Anson A. Gard, Emerson (Ottawa), 1904

United Nations Human Development Index, The United Nations (New York), 1996, 1997 & 1998

Where Rivers Meet: An Illustrated History of Ottawa, Courtney C.J. Bond, Windsor Publications (Woodland Hills, California), 1984